HESIOD'S

WORKS AND DAYS

≈≈≈≈≈

HESIOD'S
WORKS AND DAYS

~~~~~~~~~

A Translation and Commentary
for the Social Sciences by

DAVID W. TANDY *and* WALTER C. NEALE

UNIVERSITY OF CALIFORNIA PRESS
Berkeley   Los Angeles   London

University of California Press
Berkeley and Los Angeles, California

University of California Press, Ltd.
London, England

© 1996 by
The Regents of the University of California

Library of Congress Cataloging-in-Publication Data

Hesiod.
    [Works and days. English]
    Hesiod's Works and days / a translation and commentary for the
social sciences by David Tandy and Walter C. Neale.
      p. cm.
    Includes bibliographical references (p.).
    ISBN 0-520-20383-6 (alk. paper). — ISBN 0-520-20384-4
(pbk. : alk. paper)
      1. Didactic poetry, Greek—Translations into English.
    2. Agriculture—Greece—Poetry.   I. Tandy, David W.   II. Neale,
Walter C.   III. Title.
PA4010.E5T5   1996
881'.01—dc20   96-787
                                                CIP

Printed in the United States of America
9 8 7 6 5 4 3 2 1

The paper used in this publication meets the minimum requirements of
American National Standard for Information Sciences—Permanence of Paper
for Printed Library Materials, ANSI Z39.48-1984.

For A.M., M.F.T., and R.H.T.

CONTENTS

≈≈≈≈

PREFACE

This little book originated in the crossing of the authors' lives and interests. David Tandy is a classical philologist who became engaged in the study of social, economic, and political change in the eastern Mediterranean during the eighth century B.C.E. Walter Neale is an economist and economic historian who has devoted much of his life to comparative studies of social change and economic development. In 1983, when both were on the faculty of the University of Tennessee, Tandy, who had recently become acquainted with the work of Karl Polanyi, learned that Neale had been one of Polanyi's students and was leading an economic history seminar that stemmed in many ways from the work of Polanyi. Tandy became a participant in the seminar. From this experience Tandy and Neale developed an ongoing, cooperative relationship that has given rise to a number of formal and informal collaborative activities.[1]

1. These include Mayhew, Neale, and Tandy 1985; Neale and Tandy 1988; Tandy and Neale 1994. Less formal, but just as important, have been our

We undertook this translation because we were both interested in early Greece. Neale had tried repeatedly to read translations of *Works and Days;* each time he found that he had trouble understanding what Hesiod was saying about his society, and so each time he gave up the effort. When Neale learned that Tandy was translating parts of the poem for use in his social history classes, we decided to produce a version that social scientists would find easier to use than the translations currently available.

Hesiod is important because he helps us to begin understanding early Greece. But he is also important because he marks the beginning of a literary trajectory of talking about the land, a tradition continued by Xenophon in the fourth century B.C.E. Cato, Varro, and Columella took up this tradition in Rome and were known to the medieval monks who copied them. In the thirteenth century, Walter of Henley's *Houseboundrie* became the standard reference work (as it were) for farmers until John Fitzherbert's *Boke of Husbandry* was first printed in 1523. This literary tradition about the relations of people to the land continued until the shift to political economy with Adam Smith. What followed was a sentimentalized and politicized version of the tradition, exemplified well in North America, for example, by John Taylor's *Arator* in the nineteenth century and by the work of Fugitive writers like Donald Davidson and John Crowe Ransom in the twentieth. And these examples represent just the tradition of advice giving. As for

efforts in support of the Karl Polanyi Institute of Political Economy in Montreal, helping to organize the presentation of work in history and economic anthropology at the biennial conferences, examples of which have been collected in Duncan and Tandy 1994.

the relationship of the household economy to the market and the city, the situation with which Hesiod was familiar continued for generations and was, until very recently, still being duplicated in large swatches of South Asia (to which we will refer) and Latin America.

~~~~~~~~~~

The Translation

Tandy translated; Neale read. Wherever Neale had trouble understanding, he would balk, question, and suggest. We followed the obvious rule: Tandy made the final decisions about whether the Greek would bear the translation suggested by Neale. This process went on until Neale was happy. The give-and-take involved led to a proliferation of explanatory notes. These explanatory notes were written and rewritten by Tandy in response to Neale's problems and suggestions for alternative phrasings and additional commentary. Many of these notes were then incorporated into the Introduction. Neale feared that without the many readings and questions that led to his newly acquired understanding, many readers would have the same difficulties he had had earlier. However, we now both think that the present translation, with introduction and notes, makes Hesiod comprehensible at first reading.

Several concepts and terms that Hesiod uses do not translate into English at all easily. In each case the range of meanings embraces so much more in some ways and so much less in other ways that there is no clear equivalent in English. Thus, in many passages, the use of any one English word to translate a particular term would be misleading, sometimes badly misleading. We discuss major problems of translation in the Introduction (minor problems are discussed in footnotes to the text); occasionally we have inserted a footnote to the text to remind readers of the problems and to refer them to discussion in the Introduction.

We have tried hard in a number of instances to avoid taking a position on the proper English word to use in translating. Instead we provide information on the problems of finding a generally acceptable English word in order to allow readers to decide, from the context, what English equivalent they may find most appropriate in each case. In four cases (*dike, basileus, chrea,* and *kerdos*), we do not translate the Greek because these words occur so often and because the range of meanings is so varied that any English translation would be misleading; in three cases (*oikos, polis, agora*), we have retained the Greek because these terms are highly specific to ancient Greece.

In the Introduction and notes we present possible interpretations of passages and of the larger social (including economic and political) contexts. We do not mean these as in any way the correct or best interpretations. Rather, they are designed to point out possibilities that we think are likely to be overlooked by readers unfamiliar with the literature—and, as with the translation of words, we leave it to the readers to decide if the interpretation seems likely.

In our rendering of the Greek we have tried especially to be consistent and clear. One thus concedes gracefulness, though we hope that on those occasions when Hesiod is graceful we have not let him down. But we insist that this is a working translation, a tool for serious sociological analysis of a terribly important point in human history. We have followed the text of M. L. West (1978), with occasional readings from the editions of Rzach (1958 [1902]) and Solmsen (1990), from the reviews of West by Richardson (1979), Verdenius (1980), and Renehan (1980), and from the subsequent commentary by Verdenius (1985) and Renehan's review (1987). We follow West's transposition of lines 757–759 to follow 736; we do not follow West's paragraphing nor (slavishly) his punctuation. A bracketed passage, preceded by *, is one that is found in the manuscript tradition but is suspect; in this we follow West. Other brackets enclose additional information or clarification of the text.

In the notes, references to West and Verdenius by name only are to their commentaries (West 1978; Verdenius 1985).

~~~~~~~~~~~~~~~~~~

Acknowledgments

Tandy is responsible for the translation of Hesiod's *Works and Days* and translated passages from other Greek works and for all references to the literature on Greece. The authors collaborated on the Introduction and the commentary; who was primarily responsible for which parts should be obvious: each would blame the other for any errors that are present.

But we would not blame each other for coming up with the idea to put together this working translation, in which the emphasis throughout, in both introduction and commentary, is on the quotidian activities of Hesiod as agrarian producer and social critic, and on the social and economic institutions within which and in response to which these daily activities were undertaken. Hesiod's poem is a response to the arrival of a new political and economic structure in the early archaic period (750–480 B.C.E.)

and as such may be construed as a typically peasant response to pressure generated from a dominant economic center.

We would like to thank those who looked at part or all of the manuscript and offered numerous improvements, many of which we included, but, inevitably, many of which we could not accommodate: Kate Chanock, Charles Chiasson, Walter Donlan, Colin Duncan, Francis Dunn, Michael Gagarin, Cecilia Gunzberger, Thomas Hubbard, Bob Leggett, Ian Morris, James Scott, and Lee Williams. Anonymous readers for the Press also made many helpful suggestions. And James Redfield's account (1991) of the differences between classicists and anthropologists helped us through episodes of short temperament with each other.

Finally, we express our gratitude to Marian Rogers of Bibliogenesis and Mary Lamprech, editor at the University of California Press. For the art, our thanks go to Hugh A. Bailey and Seth Watson. We dedicate this with great thanks to Anne Mayhew, Mildred Tandy, and Russell Tandy.

INTRODUCTION

~~~~~~~

Works and Days is a Greek poem of 828 hexameter verses[1] that was composed in the early seventh century B.C.E. by a man named Hesiod who had a special interest in matters pertaining to agriculture: when to plant what, how to manage labor resources, and above all how to achieve productive independence (autarky) and thus to avoid hunger. In the poem Hesiod offers instruction and advice to his brother, Perses.

Hesiod's poem is important to scholars because it sheds light on the universal plight of the peasantry throughout human history; conversely, studies in peasantry help us to understand Hesiod

---

1. The earliest poetry of the Greeks was composed orally in a meter we call dactylic hexameter, each line made up of six measures (dactyls) of one long syllable followed by either two shorts or one long (the sixth measure is always either long-long or long-short). Hence the number of syllables in a line can range from twelve (very rare) to seventeen, the average being close to fifteen. Both Homer and Hesiod composed in dactylic hexameter.

and his world. Classicists and ancient historians tend to study Hesiod; other historians, sociologists, anthropologists, and economists tend to study peasants. In this work we would like to bring the ancient Greek poet-farmer more clearly into focus for social scientists and to bring some specific tools and assumptions about social organization and forms of economic integration into focus for classicists and ancient historians.

Over the years, most of the work on Hesiod, quite understandably, has been undertaken by ancient historians (with emphasis on religion and myth) and by philologists. Hesiod has always dwelt in the shadow of Homer. In fact, a standardized text of Hesiod did not appear until 1902 (Rzach 1958 [1902]). The great (and prolific) classicist Ulrich von Wilamowitz-Moellendorff published his edition and commentary on *Works and Days* in 1928, but it is not unfair to characterize this work as condescending to Hesiod and occasionally peculiar (see, for example, Wilamowitz's brief discussion of Hesiod's status in Ascra, referred to below, p. 26). Most of the best work on Hesiod in the first half of the twentieth century was undertaken by Germans, culminating in Friedrich Solmsen's influential *Hesiod and Aeschylus* (1949) and the magisterial third chapter of Hermann Fränkel's *Dichtung und Philosophie des frühen Griechentums* (1951). The generally philological focus of Hesiodic studies is exemplified by the collection of essays in the Fondation Hardt series (Reverdin 1962). Among the essays are Solmsen's "Hesiodic Motifs in Plato," Verdenius's "Aufbau und Absicht der *Erga*," and von Fritz's "Das Hesiodische in den Werken Hesiods."

Solmsen's Oxford text displaced that of Alois Rzach as the standard in 1970 (now Solmsen 1990). Martin West's indispensable edition of *Works and Days* (1978), with introduction and commentary, focuses on the dependence of the poem on the wisdom literature of the East; W. J. Verdenius's commentary (1985) on the first 382 lines focuses carefully on the text itself. Examples of more recent work along these narrowly philological lines are Robert Lamberton's *Hesiod* (1988) and Richard Hamilton's *Architecture of Hesiodic Poetry* (1989), both of which emphasize the literary merits and structure of the poem. Both are excellent studies. Although their intended audiences and their quality vary, the numerous recent translations (Lattimore 1959; Wender 1973; Athanassakis 1983; Frazier 1983; West 1988; Lombardo 1993) attest to increased interest in Hesiod. There are also very interesting new approaches to Hesiod within the discipline of classics, which we will comment on below.

Of course, Hesiod has also been studied by nonclassicists—to wit, sociologists, anthropologists, and economists—and we intend to report much of that work. Some have looked at Hesiod for a kind of validation of observations about other peasant types (e.g., Francis 1945; Redfield 1956, 107ff.). It is valuable to compare the Hesiod of *Works and Days* and the prophet Amos of the Old Testament (Andrews 1943). Karl Polanyi (1977, chap. 11) looked at Hesiod with an eye on the rise of the individual in early Greece.

THE POEM

What It Contains

Social scientists may find it helpful to view *Works and Days* as information and advice on the world and how to live in it, the information and advice being divided into three parts. The first part (1–201) is a brief history of the relations of humans with the gods, including a narrative of the degenerative series of five races, culminating in the present-day Iron Race, into which Hesiod wishes he had never been born. Hesiod offers a clear statement to the effect that living today is not as good as it used to be. There are specific but never clearly stated references to a legal problem: it seems not unlikely, perhaps even probable, that Hesiod's brother, Perses, has either brought or is bringing an action against him. If so, such circumstances help us to understand Hesiod's situation and advice later in the poem; but the first part of the poem by itself reveals little about the organization of Hesiod's society or the conduct of daily life there.

From the poem's center (202–764) one can derive a good deal of information about the organization of the society in which Hesiod lived. One can also argue ideas about what that society had been and how it was changing; but such constructs can be no more than untestable hypotheses. About what went before Hesiod we have some material evidence in the archaeological record, but textual evidence for the preceding period is limited to the Homeric epics, and interpretation of these also requires care and involves disputes. In *Works and Days* Hesiod makes remarks about what went before, but we have no way of knowing whether Hesiod's picture of the past was accurate, a nostalgic picture of the "good old days" (perhaps not unlike Homer's world of heroes in the epics), or some unknown and unknowable mixture of the two. In this introduction and in the notes in the text we present some hypotheses that we think are as plausible as others, or more plausible, but we want to stress that these are to be regarded as interpretations, not as explanations of the text.

The last part of the poem (765–828) bears little structural relation to what precedes it, and makes no mention of the details of Hesiod's world; it consists largely of advice about what to do month by month and day by day. To modern social scientists this part of the poem will appear to contain more magic than sensible advice for the farmer's quotidian rounds, but within the magic one finds much evidence about what people were doing when, and some further evidence about social organization. Again, while the import of some lines is clear (e.g., when people went on trading trips), one can only guess—or, much better, refrain from guessing—about other matters (e.g., what sort of goods were traded, and where). Throughout this part of the poem, as well as throughout the second part, we have offered many hypotheses; but, again, in each case, we have tried to indicate that we are offering possible interpretations, not explanations.

Who Composed It

The poem that came to be known by the fifth century as *Works and Days* was composed shortly after 700 B.C.E.[2] by a farmer who worked a parcel of land near Ascra, a village within the political sway of Thespiae, a *polis* (city-state) in Boeotia. Boeotia is just to the north of Athens and Attica in eastern Greece; its leading *polis* during most of antiquity was Thebes, mythically ruled long before Hesiod's lifetime by Oedipus. *Works and Days,* traditionally

2. For this date we follow Richard Janko (1982, 231).

treated as a poetic manual on farming and general husbandry, appears to be the response of one individual to changes that have occurred in his world.

During Homeric and Hesiodic times there were singers who performed at poetic competitions and at the homes of powerful men. Funeral games, such as those Achilles sponsored for Patroclus in book 23 of the *Iliad*, were regular settings for competitions, both athletic and poetic. Poetic competitions appear to have been regular aspects also of the great games at Olympia, Delphi, Isthmia, and Nemea. The annual Ionian festival at Delos featured competition in song as well. Hesiod tells us (650–659) that he won a tripod at the funeral games of Amphidamas, perhaps with his *Theogony*.

In addition to these public arenas, there were opportunities for singers in the houses of powerful men. Alcinous, king of the Phaeacians in the *Odyssey,* employs a full-time singer named Demodocus (especially book 8); Odysseus's household is regularly entertained by Phemius (who sings mostly in book 1). Demodocus and Phemius illustrate very clearly the dependence of the singer on the powerful, and they support the notion that the *Iliad* and *Odyssey* function to buttress the position of the elites in eighth-century Greek society. Hesiod's *Theogony* does so as well.

But with *Works and Days* Hesiod clearly breaks from this dependency. This change may be partly explained by his not being a narrow specialist. There are nonspecialist singers in epic: Achilles sings at *Iliad* 9.186–189; Odysseus himself sings books 9–12 of his poem. But Hesiod is not a member of their class or of their community. His dependency has been broken, perhaps by the introduction of writing.

Hesiod's other surviving poem, the *Theogony,* tells of the birth of the universe and of the gods who inhabit and rule it, but tells us little about the real world of the peasant-farmer because it was composed (probably shortly before 700, but certainly before *Works and Days*) under the same kind of constraints as Homer's *Iliad* (about 740) and *Odyssey* (about 720): that is, the *Theogony* was produced under the powerful influence of the rulers of the area in which Hesiod resided. Hence, as is the case with the Homeric epics, the *Theogony* presents a world that is governed well by gods and men; it is a poem that pays scant attention to the everyday life of those away from the center of power. *Works and Days,* by contrast, takes up precisely what is absent in those other poems, finding fault with the powerful and addressing the problems of those outside the social and economic mainstream.

Various scholars have proposed that Hesiod was a new, or at least different, type of poet, a poet who, instead of drawing from the heroic tradition from which Homer draws his material, taps a tradition of "outsider" poetry. Richard Martin noticed the similarities between Hesiod's narrative of his family's immigration to Ascra and the narrative of Phoenix's own immigration to Phthia preceding his advice to Achilles to relent in his wrath (*Iliad* 9.475– 485). Martin concludes that Hesiod offers this particular aspect of his personal history in *Works and Days* because his authority to be heard rests to some extent on his status as an outsider, "that even in its smallest details, especially those of his father's career, the *persona* of Hesiod is a *traditional* way of framing the type of 'exhortation to wisdom' poetry embodied in [*Works and Days*]" (Martin 1992, 19). That is, there appears to be a tradition in early Greece of posing as an immigrant when giving advice. Utilizing a similar approach, Ralph Rosen has ingeniously proposed that Hesiod's discussion of sailing at *Works and Days* 618–694 should not be taken literally but is intended as a metaphor for poetry and as an argument explaining that he writes Hesiodic poetry, not Homeric (epic) poetry (Rosen 1990).

Both Martin and Rosen essentially assert that Hesiod takes on a particular *persona* or poetic character. We have no objections to these proposals; but this does not mean that, for example in Martin's case, the details of Hesiod's outsider status are not in fact true (or true enough); or that, in Rosen's, Hesiod did not actually go to Chalcis and win a tripod at the funeral games of Amphidamas. And so, while these interesting readings of the poet of *Works and Days* may seem at first to threaten or compromise the verisimilitude of Hesiod's arrangements in Ascra, nevertheless at the end of the day Hesiod's world is as intact as a literal reading would suggest. We could embrace, with comfort, the outsider's stance that Hesiod takes, and would also be willing to imagine that Hesiod is describing situations that are not specifically or exactly his own; but it is important to acknowledge that the situations that Hesiod describes in his world and the conditions that are being imposed on the fields by the town are real, reflecting the world as Hesiod or "Hesiod" perceives it. As Paul Millett has put it, "It is difficult to imagine any reason why the poet should want to confuse his audience by deliberately archaizing or otherwise misrepresenting social institutions." We, too, consider *Works and Days* a "faithful formulation of Hesiod's world" (Millett 1984, 86).

Just what was this world? There is no consensus on many aspects of the early Greek world; but our attempts to understand Hesiod both contextually and literally may move us closer to understanding the Mediterranean world on the eve of classical Greek civilization. What follows is a brief overview of the prehistory of Greece, designed to help contextualize *Works and Days*.

<hr />

THE WORLD OF HESIOD'S TIME
Prehistory

In the second millennium B.C.E. there had been great centers of political and economic power throughout Greece. These were

located at many sites, now excavated, associated (by later Greeks) with the heroic leaders of later Greek myths: Agamemnon's Mycenae (after whose archaeological prominence this entire civilization is called Mycenaean), Menelaus's Sparta, Oedipus's Thebes, Theseus's Athens, and Nestor's Pylos. The importance of these centers and the complexity of their economic activities are revealed in the documents left behind on clay tablets in a syllabary of eighty-seven signs called Linear B. The tablets, found most numerously at Pylos in southwestern Greece, at Knossos on Crete, and at Thebes in Boeotia, were temporary records of accounts. They survived because they were fired when the buildings that held them were burned. The conflagrations that preserved the tablets are a clear sign that Greek civilization was undergoing a transition during this period.

Indeed, these centers began to collapse beginning about 1200. Few scholars still agree with the ancients themselves that the Mycenaean world fell victim to an invasion by Dorian Greeks from the northwest (the descendants of Heracles [= Hercules] looking for their inheritance). Some put the blame on roving bands of "Sea Peoples." Others have proposed a sudden climatic disaster. Still others have argued for a general system collapse.

The one aspect of the collapse of which we may be reasonably confident is its severity. Between about 1200 and 1000, the population of Greece appears to have been reduced by perhaps as much as three-quarters. The size of settlements became much smaller than before; the actual number of settlements was reduced by perhaps seven-eighths, from about 320 in the late thirteenth century to about 130 in the twelfth to about 40 in the eleventh (Snodgrass 1971, 364; 1980, 20). In a curious convergence of myth and archaeology, the collapse of the economic centers coincides with the mythic account of the Trojan War and of the almost universal demise of the kingdoms in mainland Greece in the war's aftermath.

From before 1000 until after 800, the Greek world stagnated. Population density remained essentially flat during this period. Contact with the outside world, which had been extensive in the Mycenaean period, came to a halt. (The Mycenaeans had had significant contacts with Egypt and the Near East; their centers faced east and south, for the most part.) The only exception was Lefkandi—we do not know its ancient name—on the large and fertile island of Euboea just off the coast of eastern Greece. It alone appears to have prospered for a while in the mid-tenth century, as increases in its population and in its contacts with outsiders indicate. This revival at Lefkandi continued until about 825. No other mainland site that defies the general pattern of darkness has been found; archaeologists have yet to find an oil lamp: it was a dark age indeed.[3]

The light at the end of this very dark tunnel appears in the first half of the eighth century, when population density appears on the rise in various locations in Greece. The most dramatic (and, predictably, the most controversial) evidence is the apparent increase in burials, at Athens and in the surrounding countryside of Attica, and in the Argolid in the east-central Peloponnese. There is argument over the size of the increase in burials between about

---

3. For good reasons the first half of the European Middle Ages is no longer referred to as the Dark Ages. However, appropriately or not, Dark Age remains the rubric for the eleventh through eighth centuries B.C.E. in Greece.

780 and about 720: according to Snodgrass, there was a sixfold increase (1977, 12; 1980, 22–23); according to Tandy, a threefold increase (1997, chap. 2; cf. Sallares 1991, 89–90). This disagreement derives from a different argument about whether selectivity[4]—at different times, certain persons were granted burial, and others were not—skewed the evidence. Others have even argued that the increase in burials indicates not more, but fewer, people.[5]

It seems fair to observe, however, that the burial counts, once adjusted for selectivity, are supported by other less arbitrary and more reliable archaeological evidence, such as an increase in the number of wells and of religious offerings at shrines to the gods. It may also be observed that there are other places—Corinth is a good example—where no great increase in burials has been observed but where similar increases in well use and settlement size are documented. We observe further that in the eighth century there are new settlements in the Aegean Sea, a pattern that should reflect the existence of more people than before. Two questions, however, still cannot be answered: Can the population increase

4. Ian Morris was able to show that until 735 only a very small percentage of those buried are infants and children, between 5 and 10 percent (Morris 1987, chap. 6 and app. 1). Suddenly after 735, infant and child burials rise to 50 to 60 percent, in the range of what palaeodemographers expect to encounter. This increase is to be explained only by a change in the treatment of infants and children. Snodgrass (1991, 15–16; 1993, 31) has now come to agree with Morris that much of the increase is attributable to the reduction in exclusivity. See further Tandy 1997, app. to chap. 2.

5. John Camp (1979) argued that a drought afflicted the Athenian settlement, leading for a time to higher mortality rates and permanently to a reduced population.

be proposed as universal throughout Greece? Did an increase in population play a role in Hesiod's world of rural Boeotia?

Even if one can argue that the population increase was smaller than what the figures we have cited suggest, there is no question or argument about whether something was going on in a number of Greek communities in the mid-eighth century. Rules were changing—rules about who got buried, about how status was distributed, and about how basic resources were made available.

An undisputed aspect of the eighth century is that outposts and colonies were founded in southern Italy and on Sicily, as Greece began to look outward again, this time to the west. Before 750 there was a Greek presence on the island of Ischia, off the coast at Naples; arguments abound over the intentions and activities of this settlement. Beginning shortly after 750, numerous settlements cropped up in southern Italy and on Sicily. Some argue that these Greeks were in the west for commercial reasons; others that these were Greeks seeking new starts. In most treatments, scholars connect the "colonizing movement" very closely with the increase in population at home. The problem here is that the very places for which we have the most dramatic evidence for growth of domestic population were *not* the mother cities of these new settlements. Athens founded none of them; Argos none. Corinth, however, was behind several, and it would appear that there was at least some increase in density there. But the leaders of the settlement at Ischia and of most of the early settlements farther to the south were the Euboeans, and it is not clear that their population was increasing at this time. The Euboeans were also the leading Greeks in the reestablishment, after several hundred years, of the port of trade at Al Mina on the Levantine coast, shortly before 800.

Al Mina, on the mouth of the Orontes River (today called the 'Asi) in northern Syria, appears to have served as the easternmost stop on a great circuit of goods transportation that stretched from there to Ischia, and then, with Phoenician help, to Marseilles and Spain. Among the many stops in between were the western "colonies" that provided Old Greece with access to foreign cultures and foreign goods to a degree unexperienced since the Mycenaean period.

More people will always present new problems to communities, and in the case of Athens the population pressure led to political reforms that eventually changed Athens into a democratic city-state. It is extremely unclear, however, how such developments to the south may have affected Hesiod and his world in central Boeotia; but Hesiod's *Works and Days* makes more sense if we keep these demographic events in mind.

We do have some thoughts about how these matters were related to Hesiod's frustration. We do not think that our ideas have affected our translation or the explanatory notes to the text. But some readers may find our ideas helpful in interpreting the implications of the text, and so we present them here, very briefly.

Before the new trade routes opened in the eighth century there was a system of interdependence between the local centers of power under *basilees* (leaders, as explained below) and the subordinate members of their communities. The leaders at the center managed the community and, among other things, settled disputes. The subordinate members supported the centers economically by contributions of goods. As well as putting the goods to their own uses, the leaders stored goods and distributed them to the other members in times of need and on other occasions. When the new trade routes opened, the leaders were the people who had enough power and resources to take advantage of the new opportunities. They were thus able further to increase their wealth and power and so became much less dependent on the subordinate members of the community. The leaders then ceased to collect goods from the subordinate members, while simultaneously ceasing to support them in times of need. (The leaders did not, however, give up their political authority.) The lack of support in times of need meant that subordinate members of the community, such as Hesiod, became dependent upon neighbors and kin (but, we will see, Hesiod does not find kin particularly dependable either). Mutually supporting relationships with people elsewhere might be established, perhaps based on trade, perhaps on gift and countergift. Since Hesiod speaks of engaging in trade and the gains to be made from it, people in his position must have participated in some kind of trade, but just how we do not know. However, they lacked the resources and power to engage in the new and rewarding long-distance trade on anything approaching the scale necessary to supplant the need for support from the centers. This lack of resources had three further consequences for those in Hesiod's position: generally increased insecurity; the possibility—in contrast to the previous system of generalized mutual obligation—of being forced into debt (see below, pp. 39–42) and thus losing all to creditors; and no release from the power of the leaders to make and enforce (perhaps irresponsible) judgments in disputes (see the discussion below on *dike,* pp. 42–48). Hence Hesiod's dejection.

Finally, what really makes a dark age dark is not the absence of lamps but the absence of writing. Linear B was a casualty of the collapse of the Mycenaean world. Before 750 a new kind of writing appears, in the alphabet that eventually evolved into those almost all Western populations use today. The alphabet likely came to the Greeks from northern Syria, probably carried by the trading Euboeans or by the Phoenicians, their partners in many of these ventures. It is impossible to account with certainty for the reintroduction of writing at this particular time; we can be fairly certain, however, that the new writing system allowed the freezing of the epic poems, both Homer's and Hesiod's.

Political Power and the basilees in the Earliest Poetry

Shortly after 750, after many years of oral composition and recomposition, the *Iliad* and the *Odyssey*, poems attributed to Homer, appear to have been frozen into the forms in which we have them.[6] These long poems, which provide a stunning starting point for the Greek literary tradition, focus on that moment in mythic time that coincides with the actual collapse of the Mycenaean world. The *Iliad* covers a few days near the end of the Trojan War; the *Odyssey* narrates the Greek hero Odysseus's return home to Ithaca. Both poems emphasize the importance of being Greek and of Greek institutions. Both poems incorporate the theme of restoration of order: the Greek warriors strive to rescue Helen of Sparta, stolen by Paris in gross violation of the rules of hospitality (*xenia*);

---

6. That is, they were either written down or were frozen in memorized form until written down in the seventh century.

Odysseus brings order back to his household by slaying virtually all the men who have taken up residence in his household and have improperly (i.e., against *xenia* rules) consumed his goods while wooing his wife.

It is clear that the epics focus on the elite stratum of society, with hardly any notice (virtually none in the *Iliad*) given to those who occupied the lower ranks. The leaders in the epics fight and speak well and do good deeds. The institutions and social relations found in the epics are consistent and probably reflect to a great extent the eighth-century world of Homer himself. Homer, of course, intends his world to be heroic, and so he endows his world with a certain otherness, although his ignorance of the Mycenaean world leads to curious results: for example, as Moses Finley (1978, 45) put it, "[Homer's] heroes lived in great palaces unknown in Homer's own day (but unlike the Mycenaean, or any other, palaces)." Homer had no idea how warriors were supposed to use chariots in battle: in the *Iliad* chariots are used by heroes as taxis to and from the field of battle.

These leaders of the Greek host at Troy, and also those in Hesiod's world, are called *basilees*. There has been, and continues to be, much discussion about the appropriate translation for the term *basileus* (pl. *basilees*); there is no generally accepted rendering. "King," "*roitelet*," "baron," "lord," "big man," and "head man" are each suitable in some ways, but unsuitable in others.

During the Dark Age, the semblance of a political center appears to have been provided by the *basileus,* a vestige of the Mycenaean age, when the *qa-si-re-u* was a relatively unimportant intermediary between the outermost political periphery and the *wanax* (roughly, "lord"),[7] at the center of an elaborate redistributive system. It seems likely that the *basilees* had been mere heads of villages. The destruction of the Mycenaean centers brought power to the leaders of these newly independent communities: after the Mycenaean collapse, there were only villages, and *basileus* became the rubric of power (Thomas 1978, 191; Drews 1983, 112–14; Fine 1983, 25; Carlier 1984, 108–16).

The *basilees* at Troy are loosely confederated under Agamemnon's leadership. Recent studies of *basilees* at Troy in the *Iliad* (Lenz 1993; Ulf 1990) and on Ithaca in the *Odyssey* (Halverson 1985, 1986) demonstrate the subtle ways in which the pecking order among the *basilees* is established and readjusted periodically. On the magical island of Scheria in the *Odyssey,* things are more organized, and Alcinous seems more than *primus inter pares.* Meetings of the island's *basilees* take place in his house, and it is Alcinous who announces municipal outlays and presumably has the power to "tax" his people when resources are needed (discussed below, p. 22).

We might profitably compare the system in India before the British. There were less- and more-powerful rulers who held sway over political entities as small as villages and as large as provinces and who enjoyed a wide variety of titles (e.g., *maharaja, nizam, diwan,* for larger areas; *raja, jagidar, talukdar,* for smaller areas). The regions dominated by these rulers were often, in principle,

7. The Greek term *wanax* is used of supreme commanders in the *Iliad* and is one of two rubrics of paramountcy in the Linear B tablets (the other is *la-we-ge-tas,* "people leader"). The term resists etymology and is presumed by most scholars to be a foreign borrowing, as *basileus* also is.

parts of a larger empire, but each ruler tried to be as independent as he could be and was only as loyal and obedient as he had to be.[8]

The Pidgin English for such institutionalized positions of power in many societies—often a reasonable translation from the vernacular—is "big man" (a variant of which, familiar to readers of stories about India, is *burra sahib,* "big lord"). In their African empire the British called such people chiefs. However, "big man" always strikes people as a bit silly or even condescending, and "chief" carries a connotation of a backward or uncivilized society. "Baron," suggested by Peter Green (1984, 28 n. 33), is as good a word as we can find in English, although to us "baron" implies the European feudal system and doctrines. Unlike a baron, the *basileus* did not depend on an overlord for the grant of power (or land) and took no oaths of homage and fealty.

Any practical definition of the *basilees* would have to begin with the warning: "Don't mess around with them!"

There was a time when Hesiod approved of the *basilees:*

> Sweet words flow from the mouth of a *basileus.* All the people watch him as he decides law cases with straight *dikai;* and even he, speaking surely, would put a stop to a great wrangling. For therefore there are *basilees* with wise hearts, for when the people are being misled in the *agora,* they easily settle cases that might bring harm, moving them with soothing words. When he goes through the assembly, they greet

8. For accounts of such people in Oudh (in northern India) in the nineteenth century, see Baden-Powell 1892 and Neale 1962. For an account of the system in Maharashtra (on the Deccan plateau in western India) during the two or three centuries before British conquest—and the importance of conditional loyalty in Islamic and Hindu thought—see Wink 1986.

him as a god with sweet reverence, and he is conspicuous among those gathered. (*Theogony* 84–92)

It has been noted how similar these sentiments are to those found in the *Odyssey,* and that Hesiod uses the same language that Odysseus uses to describe a "good" leader: "He carefully addresses them with sweet reverence, and he is conspicuous among those gathered, and when he goes through the town, they look at him as a god" (*Odyssey* 8.171–173; see further Martin 1984). In the *Theogony* Hesiod speaks, as Homer does, of *basilees* as consistently good. In Homer, leaders *are* good, and for that reason people flourish, as we see in these remarks by the disguised Odysseus to his wife, Penelope:

> Your fame reaches broad heaven, just like that of a blameless
> *basileus,* who god-fearing and ruling over many and mighty
> men upholds good *dike* (*eudikie*), and the black earth bears
> wheat and barley, trees are heavy with fruit, flocks give birth
> continuously, and the sea bears forth fishes, all thanks to his
> good leadership, and the people prosper under him. (*Odyssey*
> 19.108–114)

The world of *Works and Days* is different, however. On the one hand, it is still the case that communities will prosper under excellent leadership:

> But those who give straight *dikai* to outsiders and insiders
> and do not diverge at all from what is just, for them the *polis*
> thrives, and the people in it bloom. And Peace, who nurtures
> children, is throughout the land; Zeus the Wide-Viewer never
> assigns painful war to them. And never do Hunger or Calam-
> ity attend upon men of straight *dikai,* but they enjoy at festivi-

ties the fruits of the works they have tended. For them the earth bears much sustenance, and in the mountains the oak bears acorns on top and bees in the middle. Their woolly sheep become heavy all over from their fleeces; women bear children that resemble their parents. They thrive with good things continually. And therefore they do not go onto ships, but the grain-giving plowland bears [enough] produce [every year]. (225–237)

But it is also the case now that the *basilees* cannot be counted on to be so virtuous, as Hesiod immediately turns to another kind of behavior:

> To those whose care is evil violence and cruel works Zeus the Wide-Viewer, the son of Cronus, assigns *dike*. Many times even the entire *polis* fares ill for an evil man who commits offenses and plots actions of outrage. On them the son of Cronus brings a great disaster from heaven: hunger and plague together. The people die; women do not give birth; *oikoi* become diminished by the ploys of Olympian Zeus. At different times in turn the son of Cronus destroys their wide army, or their wall, or exacts atonement from their ships upon the open sea. (238–247)

Thus does Hesiod abandon any support for the ideology of the early *polis,* an ideology that includes the notion of equality among all those allowed to participate as citizens but also the notion of the virtues of a centralized leadership that acts on behalf of the citizen body, regardless of the form of government (democracy, oligarchy, tyranny). Above all, the Greek *polis* was a citizen-state from its earliest appearance in the eighth century (see further Raaflaub 1993, 42–46).

Until about Hesiod's time, much, perhaps most, of the production and provisioning of goods was centrally organized in redistributive systems wherein people contributed a good deal, even all, of their production to a center and received back a great variety of goods and services, including feasts and festivals. This was certainly the case during the Mycenaean period and probably the case, on a reduced scale, throughout the Dark Age.

In the *Odyssey,* on the island of Scheria, a centralized, redistributive system appears the norm. Alcinous, a *basileus* on Scheria, tells us that "twelve distinguished *basilees* rule throughout the people (*demos*) as rulers, and I am the thirteenth" (*Odyssey* 8.390–391). Of course, the very existence of this strong central group of thirteen leaders may or may not imply redistribution, but we are reminded of Solomon's Israel of the ninth century: "And Solomon had twelve officers over all Israel, which provided victuals for the king and his household: each his month a year made provision" (1 Kings 4.7). When Odysseus is about to leave Scheria, Alcinous publicly announces: "But come now, let us give him a great tripod and a caldron, each man of us; in turn we will get requital by taking a collection throughout the people (*demos*): it is a hard thing for one man to make a proper gift from his own gift store" (*Odyssey* 13.13–15). Thus Alcinous and the other leaders are able to recoup their "loss" by taxing the people and will be able to continue to do so as long as it does not appear unfair or avoidable. In these cases, goods move into a central location, and then other goods, or services, move out in turn to the periphery.

While Odysseus is wandering the world, suitors of his wife,

Penelope, are consuming the materials of his household. One player in this arrangement is Eumaeus the swineherd, whose responsibility it is to supply the household of Odysseus with swine; his ability to do this has allowed him to maintain his livelihood both before Odysseus left for the war and during the subsequent occupation of Odysseus's household by the suitors of Penelope. Eumaeus himself tells us that "I myself keep and tend these swine and choose the best of the boars and send it to the suitors" (*Odyssey* 14.107–108). However fond he is of the absent Odysseus, it appears to matter little for Eumaeus's activities who occupies the center.

By Hesiod's time, trade had become important, but we do not know just how it was conducted. About ports of trade we can be fairly sure; about long-distance trade we know a good deal, as indicated in our account of Greek colonies in the discussion of population above. However, about trade over shorter distances and on a smaller scale we can only make some guesses based on a few clues.

Markets in early Greece were for the most part peripheral, by which we mean simply that very few persons depended on markets for their basic needs (food, clothing, and shelter). In addition, most markets in antiquity were controlled, characteristically by the government.[9] Good examples of ancient controlled markets

9. If the inscription executed in 409/8 in Athens of Draco's law on homicide is faithful to the original legislation of about 620, then we have a reference to a peripheral market a mere fifty or so years after Hesiod's *Works and Days*. In the inscription an ancient Athenian could read a reference to the *agora ephoria,* the "border market," the "border" in this case referring to political boundaries between city-states.

were those of Babylonia and Assyria, where prices were fixed[10] and on which, in fact, few depended for their livelihoods. In the ancient emporia, such as Tilmun (Bahrain) and Al Mina, mostly luxury and prestige goods were transferred (for Tilmun see, for example, Oppenheim 1954; for Al Mina see Tandy 1997, chap. 3). The prophet Ezekiel gives a vivid image of the port of trade at Tyre, cataloging for us the fine goods from faraway places that were exchanged (Ezekiel 27; see further Polanyi 1960, 343–45; Tandy and Neale 1994, 15).

About food markets we know little. They probably arose spontaneously as one-time ("spot") markets during times of natural disaster.[11] There is a description in the *Iliad* of such a one-time market when ships pulled into the harbor at Troy:

> Many ships from Lemnos were at hand carrying wine, ships
> that Jason's son Euneos had sent out; Hypsipyle had borne
> Euneos to Jason, shepherd of the people. And only to the
> Atreidae, Agamemnon and Menelaus, had Jason's son given
> wine to carry off, one thousand measures. From this source
> the flowing-haired Achaeans got wine, some by [exchanging]
> bronze, some by shining iron, some by hides, some by whole
> oxen, some by slaves. (*Iliad* 7.467–475)

---

10. "[The] institution of markets . . . was in Mesopotamia clearly of limited and marginal importance" (Oppenheim 1977, 385 n. 13); cf. Polanyi 1957.

11. There is a terrific example from ancient Egypt: a woman accused of stealing gold that was found in her house defended herself by asserting: "I got it selling barley in the year of the hyenas, when everyone was short of food" (Montet 1981, 71, 267). This is clear testimony to a one-time market, not (*pace* Silver 1983, 798; 1986, 78) evidence of quotidian self-regulating markets.

It may have been to such markets, rather than to ports of trade, that Hesiod took or shipped his goods.

Clearly trade was growing important, as were markets, but neither the trade nor even a single one of the markets should ever be treated as part of a self-regulating market system (often assumed by economic historians but never actually existing there).[12]

~~~~~~~~~~~~

HESIOD'S DAILY BREAD

What Hesiod is most concerned about is getting enough to eat. He has practical concerns along these lines and spends quite a bit of time on them.

Hesiod the Farmer

Hesiod worked a parcel of land (Greek *kleros,* "lot") on which was situated an economic organization called an *oikos,* for which up to this point we have been using the word "household." An *oikos* (pl. *oikoi*) comprised a piece of land and all the buildings on it, the animals and people who lived on it, and the productive means used to generate subsistence for all who belonged to it. The lot could be divided among sons by inheritance, which appears to be what happened to Hesiod and his brother, Perses, upon the death of their father, who had moved to Ascra from Cume in Greek Asia Minor:

12. Elsewhere Tandy has developed some models for market types as they may have existed in early Greece. See Tandy 1997, chaps. 4 and 5.

My father and yours . . . used to sail in ships, because he was in need of a good livelihood. Once he came here in his black ship, after making it across much open sea, having left behind Aeolian Cume. He was not fleeing riches, wealth, and prosperity, but the evil poverty that Zeus gives to men. He settled near Helicon in a pitiful village, Ascra, bad in the winter, painful in the summer, never any good. (633–640)

It is not the weather that Hesiod is complaining about; in order to understand Hesiod's complaint we have to look elsewhere.

We follow Paul Millett (1984, 107), who, drawing on Robert Redfield's broad definition of peasant (1953, 31), concludes that Hesiod fits the picture well. We also recommend to the reader the intelligent survey of the more recent peasant literature in Victor Magagna's *Communities of Grain* (1991, 1–24).

Although it seems rather obvious to many of us that Hesiod is most efficiently studied as a peasant or smallholder, there have been efforts to make him something else. We summarize some of these arguments here. Benedetto Bravo (1977) argues that Perses and Hesiod were, like their father before them, impoverished *aristoi,* the term used by Homer and other early poets to describe the "best men." Alfonso Mele (1979) sees Hesiod as a representative of this aristocracy, advocating among other things the propriety of nonprofessional "trade" by the *aristoi.* We dismiss two other positions because there is really no evidence to support them: Chester Starr's modernizing portrait of Hesiod and of his father as "semi-aristocrats" (1977, 125–27; cf. 1982, 432–33, 434; 1986, 93–94) and Wilamowitz-Moellendorff's speculation that Hesiod's father was a non-*aristos* who, when he came to Ascra,

fooled the locals into thinking that he was a descendant of Boeotian *aristoi* who had emigrated to Aeolis (1928, 76).

Hesiod's oikos *and Livelihood*

Hesiod's farm was part of his *oikos* and was worked by members
of his *oikos;* his neighbors in and around the village of Ascra
formed some sort of community of such households, each of
which existed independently of the others. To the extent that it
was possible, the community appears to have been independent
of the *polis* (Thespiae) and its authority.

Hesiod engaged in what we would now call mixed farming. He
grew grains, plowing with oxen (436) and asses (46, 607), tended
vines, and kept livestock, the same trio of productive categories
that we find in Homer's description of a farm in the *Iliad* (14.122–
124). He may also have kept livestock on "public" ("common")
lands, to judge from his reference to eating the meat of a cow "fed
in the woods" (591). But Hesiod's advice is mainly about pro-
ducing grain.

Size of Hesiod's Farm

We cannot know the size of Hesiod's farm, or of the farms of other
oikoi in his community, but we can estimate a range of size, using
bits of evidence from other times and places and rules of thumb.
The range is large, but the farm was small by modern European,
to say nothing of modern North American, standards.

We may start with the proposition that when the staple diet
is grain, an adult will consume up to but no more than 16 to
18 ounces of food grain. This diet is sufficient for survival but

leaves the person easily subject to disease and certainly does not provide enough to allow the person to work hard. However, once people are consuming this much grain they do not want to eat more grain; rather, they want to supplement the grain with other foodstuffs: milk, curds, whey, cheese, oils, vegetables, roots, fruit, meat. While it is clear from the tenor of Hesiod's comments on the threats of hunger and debt that his *oikos* is not well-to-do, neither does he appear to be dirt-poor: he has slaves, he hires people, and he speaks of sending goods off for trade. His *oikos* thus appears to be bigger (and relatively better-to-do) than our typical picture of an eighteenth- or nineteenth-century peasant household but far short of an "estate"—and so it is also fair to assume that his farm produces enough grain to feed the people on his *oikos* with some to spare.

How many people were there in his *oikos?* Presumably he has a wife, since he appears to have at least one son (271, 376–377); this makes three people. If we assume that Hesiod has followed his own good advice, then we can say several things about his *oikos.* Among the residents is a slave woman who follows his plow and keeps his house in order, although the text is unreliable (405–406; see note 93 there). There is another woman (or the same one?) who does the chores in the house (603–604). A forty-year-old male laborer does some of the plowing (441–446); and he or another man follows the plow as he covers the seeds (469–471). This adds another two to four people. Hesiod hires on an occasional worker (*thes,* pl. *thetes*) from outside his *oikos,* who would have been resident for limited periods. (*Thetes* are the lowest caste in early Greece. They do not belong anywhere; even slaves belong to an *oikos.* In Hesiod's *oikos, thetes* are thrown out when their work is no longer needed. See lines 600–603 and note 150.) Hesiod also occasionally hires a friend (370), who we may presume is never resident. Hesiod has slaves (at least two?) who build granaries (502–503), help with the reaping (573) and processing (597), and plow the field for fallow after the harvest (607–608). Thus we find seven to nine people mentioned as permanent residents. Hesiod may have other sons, a daughter or daughters, and more than two slaves.

Let us guess that an *oikos* such as Hesiod's supported ten or twelve adult equivalents, each consuming some 400 pounds of food grains a year, requiring a total of some 4,000 to 4,800 pounds of grain annually. To this quantity we need to add a sixth for seed and some unknown amount to supplement the grazing and fodder diets of working oxen and donkeys and for lactating cows (whether nursing or milk-yielding), and perhaps a bit for other livestock. Hesiod's *oikos* would thus need upwards of 6,000 pounds of grain each year. However, Hesiod may also have grown more for storage against the threat of crop failure (see below, under "Storage"). Hesiod also speaks of sending goods out in trade (see below); we do not know what goods, but grain is one possibility.

Yields are hard to estimate. The fertility of the soil, the soil's ability to retain water, natural drainage, the amount and distribution of rainfall over the growing season, number of plowings, intensity of cultivation (weeding, loosening of soil)—all these factors affect yields, and Hesiod gives us no clues to judge these matters. In modern Boeotia land generates 9 to 12 bushels (570 to 770 pounds) per acre. After two centuries of low population density, land in Hesiod's day may have recovered a good deal of its natural fertility; on the other hand, the plows were probably less effective and the oxen smaller.[13] For one district in northern India—not Greece, but where a similar ox-plow technology was used on well-worn soils—estimated yields varied from 350 pounds per acre for millets (grown on poor ground) to 620 pounds for wheat during the third and fourth decades of the nineteenth century. For the first two decades of the twentieth century the estimates ranged from 450 pounds for millets to 1,000 pounds for barley.

If we estimate yields on Hesiod's land at 600 pounds per acre—always remembering we may be overestimating by a half or underestimating by a third—then he would have needed about 10 acres under a grain crop each year. This is consistent with the rule of thumb that a man and pair of oxen can manage about 5 acres of arable (land for cropping). More acres would be possible if the soils were light or if only the surface inches were "scratch" plowed. If Hesiod used a three-field system—in which a third of the land is left fallow (uncultivated) to recover each year—he would have needed 15 acres of arable. If he used a two-field system—in which half the land is left fallow each year—his total arable would have been about 20 acres (or more, if he grew for storage or trade). Then we should allow some additional acreage for vegetables (which Hesiod does not mention), vines, and some olive and fruit trees. Hesiod's *oikos* thus contained 25, and perhaps more than 30, acres. While this is a significantly larger property than the 15 acres estimated as the standard farm size for the

13. For the modern data see Bintliff 1985, 210. But the relationship between ancient and modern (but premechanized) yields is extremely thorny. See Halstead 1987; Halstead and Jones 1989, 54; Garnsey 1992, 149.

seventh century and later (Cooper 1977–78, 169; Andreyev 1974, 14–16), we must keep in mind that there were many more people later, in Boeotia and elsewhere. Even if we overestimate Hesiod's holding by a sizeable amount, we must also keep in mind that Hesiod's father's *oikos* was twice the size of Hesiod's, a reflection of a time when there were even fewer people in the area. We should also point out that Hesiod's narrative implies that his family did not occupy the best land in the area.

In any case, Hesiod does not think that his *oikos* is overpopulated: "Easily would Zeus give unquenchable prosperity to more persons. The care of more hands is more, and the increase is greater" (379–380). This is a sensible position, taking the good years with the bad, so long as there was still unused land that could be brought into his holding and under the plow.

Tools and Equipment

At lines 420–435, Hesiod offers instruction on picking out different woods of differing sizes and shapes for the construction of three different things: a mortar and pestle, a wagon, and a plow. The most detailed information Hesiod provides is about the plow. During the Dark Age people's staple diet was probably the olive, and the plow disappeared from use. The account of the appropriate woods and their joints and joinings may have appealed to Hesiod's audience because the plow was, to them, a new and even exciting implement.

We are of the opinion that Hesiod's plow had an iron plowshare, because of the likelihood that the property that Hesiod inherited from his father had to be cleared and turned for the first time when Hesiod's father arrived from Aeolis. Hesiod does not mention the iron share, but his preoccupation with the different parts of the wooden structure of the plow may explain this omission (Gow 1914, 266 n. 49). No iron plowshare from ancient Greece has been found anywhere (Schiering 1968, 151), no doubt because the iron was recycled into a new share. The *Iliad* may provide good evidence for both the iron plowshare and the recycling of its material. When Achilles offers a prize of rough-cast iron at the funeral games of Patroclus, he says of its winner:

> He will have it for five full years to use,[14] for not for lack of iron will the shepherd or the plowman go into the *polis*, but this will provide it. (*Iliad* 23.833–835)

The utility of iron to the plowman is clear; it is difficult to imagine how the shepherd might use it, though knives and axes are made of iron in Homer. Of course, this may simply indicate that a worker (shepherd or plowman) routinely went to town to do errands on behalf of the *oikos*. Note that not only does the passage imply the use of an iron plowshare; it more clearly suggests that iron was not so easy to come by.

During plowing time, Hesiod or his men use a mattock to cover the seeds (470) and a mallet to break the clods (425); they use sickles for reaping (775) and for cutting vines (573); Hesiod oversees his own threshing on a threshing floor (599), for which he needs a winnow; grinding is done with wooden mortar and pestle (423). There is a loom to produce textiles (538, 779); Hesiod has a way to cut felt (542); he also needs a tool for castrating live-

---

14. The limit refers not to how long it will last, but how long it may be used before being returned to Achilles.

stock (786, 790–791). Other equipment that Hesiod mentions includes wagons (426, 453, 692) and a steering oar (45, 629), which he keeps over his fireplace (and hopes never to use).

Hunger, Crop Failure, and Debt

Hesiod is very concerned with hunger (*limos*) and avoiding it: he mentions hunger no fewer than seven times in *Works and Days*, twice (404, 647) linking it with the other great dread that will not go away: *chrea*, "debts" (about which we will say much more below). He associates it with poor husbandry; but, as we are coming to understand it (Garnsey 1988, 8–16; Garnsey and Morris 1989; Halstead 1989), interannual variability of rainfall in Greece must have resulted in very frequent crop failure, with great variability from region to region every year and great variability from year to year in every region of Greece: good reason to fear hunger. However, Hesiod never refers to crop failure as a cause of hunger and debt, although he does emphasize the importance of filling one's granary. (Perhaps because the poem chastises his brother for poor husbandry, he offers only good husbandry as a solution: after all, he cannot blame Perses for a lack of rain, although he does associate good yields with the moral behavior of the *basilees* [225 237].) Still, readers may ask themselves whether storage or getting grain from elsewhere might not have allowed fairly easy survival in a single year, perhaps longer.

Storage

The threat of hunger could be much reduced by storing in good years against crop failure in bad. Hesiod speaks of building granaries (502–503); he advises his listeners to leave the majority of one's production behind when moving the rest by ship (689–690). Typically grain was stored in *pithoi* (sing. *pithos*). These large (up to six feet high), thick-sided, sometimes immobile jars (whose shape changed little over millennia) could store grain without spoilage for up to three years. In the second millennium B.C.E., they were used in great numbers at the palaces at Knossos and Pylos. Some have been found at Dark Age sites. But, curiously, Homer and Hesiod mention *pithoi* as storage containers only for wine (although we cannot be sure that by *pithos* they refer to the same pot shape that modern archaeologists call a *pithos: Odyssey* 2.340, 23.305; *Works and Days* 368, 815, 819).[15]

We have models of special-design, freestanding granaries from an Athenian burial dated to about 850 B.C.E. (Smithson 1968, 92–97) and from eighth-century burials in Athens (Smithson, 92 n. 41, nos. 2–10). If late eighth-century foundations discovered at Lefkandi (Popham and Sackett 1968, 30–31, figs. 69–70; Popham, Sackett, and Themelis 1980, pls. 5–7, 8b) are in fact foundations of granaries (the excavators first thought that they were wine-presses), each may have held as many as 450 bushels of grain, or enough to feed more than 60 adults for a year. There is what appears to be a very large storage building dating from the eighth century at Old Smyrna, but it is not certain that it was intended for grain storage (Akurgal 1983, 28; building J in figs. 14, 15, and 18a [a reconstruction reproduced also in Coldstream 1977, 305,

15. Homer also tells us of the two *pithoi* in Zeus's house, one containing good things that he distributes to mortals, the other containing evils (*Iliad* 24.527–528); Hesiod tells us that it was from a *pithos* that Pandora released all the evils into the world (*Works and Days* 94–99).

fig. 96b]; pl. 17). All this evidence indicates that sizeable amounts of grain were being stored, but these granaries seem entirely too large for an *oikos* the size of Hesiod's.

Getting Grain from a Distance

Another possible defense against hunger is the acquisition of grain from some distance, either by gift[16] or by some sort of market exchange. But about this Hesiod tells us nothing. He speaks of shipping (unidentified) goods, but always in an "outward-bound" direction, and always for the gain to be made from shipping them. If this suggests that Hesiod, when he *had* a surplus of production, could always find a place to carry it (or to send it), it opens the questions of whether he could have brought grain in from a distance, and if he did not, why he did not. Certainly Hesiod strongly emphasizes dependence on the goodwill of local neighbors in times of need; so there may have been some barrier to getting grain from a distance.

Hesiod's Trading

Daily life in Hesiod's Boeotia contrasts sharply with the day-to-day life that we glimpse in the Homeric epics. In Hesiod's Boeotia surplus production does not go to a central place for storage and redistribution. Rather, Hesiod takes his goods to sea (probably to the port of Kreusis, about twenty miles away) to be carried by

16. This is a possibility even over substantial distances. In locally bad years people in Tivland (in central Nigeria) "send hunger"—namely, requests for food—to distant relatives who might live as far away as relatives, friends, or mutually supportive "partners" in Greece could have lived (see Bohannan and Bohannan 1968, 143).

ship either to a port of trade or to a peripheral, one-time market. Hesiod advises his listeners to "praise a little ship, but put your cargo in a big one: the greater the cargo, the greater will be the *kerdos*[17] on top of *kerdos,* if the winds hold back the evil blasts" (643–645). It is curious that the only risks that Hesiod envisions are "evil blasts"; he makes no mention of prices. If the destination of Hesiod's goods is a port of trade, his lack of worry about prices lends some support to the view that prices were fixed at ports of trade (see Revere 1957; Polanyi 1963). However, if Hesiod's goods are destined to a one-time market, the lack of worry about prices could also be attributable to either of two causes: one-time markets arise only in response to local shortages, and thus prices will be high; or, since all of Hesiod's costs have been absorbed within his *oikos,* any price will be a gain.

A final point on the destination of Hesiod's goods: Hesiod himself would not necessarily need (or want) to know where his goods would be headed before he reached Kreusis. A port of trade's address may have remained constant, but interannual rain variations will have created one-time markets almost every year, with locations changing almost every year as well.

More important, however, than the identification of the precise kind of destination to which Hesiod's goods are traveling, is the recognition that the goods are being taken outside rather than being delivered somewhere within the sort of redistributive formation that we must surmise for the world of Eumaeus. The mechanism for transferring surplus goods *within* the community has

17. *Kerdos* means "gain" in the broadest of senses and seems to be the obverse of *chreos,* which means "debt" in the broadest of senses.

been replaced by a mechanism *outside* the community. Furthermore, the goal of such movements is to increase as much as one can one's own *kerdos,* a gain for oneself in contrast to a gain on behalf of the community (see note 76 on *kerdos*).

What has not changed are the relations among neighboring *oikoi,* which are clearly still reciprocal. Among many examples is the following: "Take good measure from a neighbor, and pay it back well, with the same measure, *or better* if you can, so that you may later find him reliable should you need him" (349–352; our emphasis). This is a classic example of the necessity of apparent generosity in reciprocal relations (see note 83). Sharing and maintaining neighborly relations are recurrent themes throughout *Works and Days;* the collapse of the redistributive formation has done little to undermine reciprocal relations away from the political center. In fact, we suspect that the collapse of the political center as economic center probably has strengthened these mutual dependencies, since community- or class-awareness begins to emerge (see Magagna 1991, 12–21) as the peripheral—both geographical and social/political/economic—members of the Greek communities begin to perceive their plight.

We are left to conclude that Hesiod's world is without an economic center that benefits those in Hesiod's position, and that Hesiod and his neighbors are forced to fend for themselves by banding together and aspiring to autarky within their independent *oikoi.*

A Farmer's Almanac

Hesiod's specific advice about what to do at what times of year adds up collectively to what may be called his farmer's almanac.

Outline of Hesiod's Annual Activities

(Adapted from West 1978, 253)

Our Months	Celestial Phenomena[18]	Seasonal Events	Farming Activities	Lines
Sept.	Sirius up mostly at night	Rains begin	Woodcutting	419ff.
Oct.				
Nov.	Pleiades setting	Cranes migrate	Plowing	384 448ff.
	Orion setting			619ff.
Dec.	Solstice		Late plowing	479ff.
Jan.	Lenaion (name of the month)			504ff.
Feb.	Arcturus rising at twilight	Swallow seen	Vine pruning	564ff.
Mar.				
Apr.	Pleiades hidden			385ff.
May	Pleiades rising	Fig leaves growing	Sailing Harvest	678ff. 383ff. 571ff.
Jun.	Solstice		Threshing	597ff.
Jul.	Sirius rising Orion rising	Thistle in bloom	Drinking	582ff.
Aug.	Etesian winds		Sailing	663ff.
Sept.	Arcturus rising at dawn; Sirius and Orion due south		Grape harvest	609ff.

~~~~~~~~~~~~~

18. West has a very useful appendix on risings and settings of stars (West 1978, 376–81). Bickerman (1980, 51–56) is helpful as well. The best rule of thumb is that when Hesiod mentions a rising or setting he is probably referring to a rising or setting just before dawn; less often he means a rising or setting in the early evening.

In this section, we want to lay out fully the players in the narrative drama of *Works and Days* and the rules behind many of the players' behaviors and behind Hesiod's remarks. We have already discussed interneighbor reciprocity. Now we turn to the actions taken by outsiders that are driven by new rules coming out from the town.

Chrea

Hesiod addresses *Works and Days* to his brother, Perses, who appears to have lost his *oikos*. There are inconsistencies in the depiction of Perses's situation, but we can be sure of this much: Perses has lost his land because he accumulated too many debts (*chrea* at 404, 647), a new social notion that also indicates the absence of a redistributive system, within which we would ordinarily expect an individual to owe only as much as he can pay. Perses appears to have encumbered his own holding (*kleros*) with *chrea* until he lost it.

Chrea are obligations of many sorts. *Chrea* include what we think of as debts (in the widest sense) but also much more—more even than is implied in the American vernacular expression "Now you owe me one."

Louis Gernet observed that in the Greek language *chreos* "is applied to a global notion in which there appear . . . four related ideas: the idea of a constraint that weighs on the debtor; the idea of an obligation that is punishable in case of default; the idea of the very thing that, once received, 'obligates'; the ideas, in addition, of propriety, duty, and even religious observation" (Gernet 1981, 147).

Some of the breadth of connotation for *chreos* (also spelled *chreios*) can be seen in Homer. Odysseus's absence has brought about a *chreios* for Telemachus (*Odyssey* 2.45). Ares acquires a *chreios* when he is caught in flagrante with Aphrodite (*Odyssey* 8.353, 355). The Trojans fear that the Achaeans will pay them back a *chreios* for the defeat the Trojans administered to them the day before (*Iliad* 13.746); similarly, *chreios* is used to describe the motivations of the Pylians' and Eleans' recurring raids of each other (*Iliad* 11.686, 688, 698) and, likewise, to describe Odysseus's trip to Messene to collect a *chreos* after the Messenians took 300 head of sheep from Ithaca (*Odyssey* 21.17). These last two examples illustrate obligations resulting from robbery and rustling.

Finally, there are two uses that appear to refer to debt pure and simple (to the extent that there is such a thing), and so mirror the uses in Hesiod: Eurymachus the suitor asks Telemachus whether Mentes the Taphian trader (Athena in disguise) was visiting Ithaca to see to a *chreios* (*Odyssey* 1.409); Mentes/Athena says later that he/she is off to visit the Cauconians, "where a *chreios* is owed me" (*Odyssey* 3.367). From this we reason that one man's *chreos* can become another man's *kerdos* (discussed above). And this kind of *chreos* appears, from the context of Hesiod's remarks, to be of a new type that can be accumulated against one's land, because too many *chrea* threaten the loss of land. A *chreos* used to be a continuing obligation; now a *chreos* has become collectible and can force foreclosure of land.

Chrea are more than mere vexations. In both of his explicit references to *chrea* (404, 647), Hesiod links *chrea* with *limos,* "hunger," and clearly at 404–405 Hesiod connects *chrea* to Perses' loss of his *oikos* and his livelihood. We reason further from the whole drift of Hesiod's argument that the defense against too many *chrea* is to accumulate *kerdea*.

Later, in Athens, *chrea* led to debt slavery, the abolition of which by Solon's legislative reforms of about 594 B.C.E. may be read as the beginning of a trend that led to democracy in the form of Cleisthenes' reforms in 508. Thus *chrea* had the unintended but salutary effect of leading to the institutionalization of democracy at Athens; no such eventuality ever occurred in Boeotia.

Hesiod encourages Perses to rid himself of *chrea* by pursuing the accumulation of *kerdea:* as we saw above, a successful trading venture will bring "*kerdos* on top of *kerdos*" (644). Thus we may surmise that *kerdea* are a defense against the *chrea* that can lead to the loss of one's land. Industry leads to autarky; autarky together with *kerdea* can prevent the harm that *chrea* can bring. Since it would appear that Perses lost his land to those who held sway in Thespiae, we may conclude that autarky and *kerdea* are cultural and economic defensive weapons aimed narrowly at the once-redistributive center that has been transformed into something new.

Before moving on, it is appropriate to make reference to the important work of Edouard Will and Marcel Detienne, who argued that since land is not alienable (that is, transferable through sale), the accumulation of debts leads not to the loss of the property but to the loss of control of production. The agrarian crisis, as Detienne called it, originates "in the practice of successive divisions, a practice that was the result of the breakdown of the primitive family" (Will 1957, 17). Sons of a smallholder have a choice whether to divide their inherited property or not, but because of the inferiority of the holding (because of population pressure), divided or not, they are on occasion forced to borrow from a neighbor, usually a wealthy one. A series of bad harvests leads to the debtor being "sucked down little by little into even greater misery. From loan to loan, he will finally be forced to 'sell' his plot of land" (Detienne 1963, 25–26). But, says Will, land is not alienable, and so all that the wealthy *aristos* can accomplish is eventually to gain complete control over the smallholder's production. Although title is not ceded to the *aristos,* in effect the land no longer belongs to the indebted smallholder. Over time, the production on more and more holdings comes under the control of the wealthy families (Detienne, 26).

Will's and Detienne's work is important and attractive, but we cannot see how one can avoid concluding that Perses' land has been literally separated from him. Perses has no *oikos;* he has no *kleros.*

Dike

However interpreted, some kind of legal action by Perses against Hesiod is the starting point of the poem:

> Right here let us settle our wrangling (*neikos*) with straight *dikai,* which are from Zeus and best. For we had already distributed the holding, but you snatched and carried off many other things, energetically feeding the pride of gift-eating *basilees,* who are willing to offer a *dike* in this case. (35–39)

Dike (pl. *dikai*) in *Works and Days* seems to have a primary meaning of "settlement, judgment," when it refers to a judge's ruling (39, 219, 221, 225, 264), or "plea," when it refers to a contestant's position (36), or both (230, 250, 254, 262). It can also refer to the size of the settlement (272) and to the actual settlement offered by one party to the other (712). In *Works and Days* these *dikai* are routinely either "straight" (good) or "crooked" (bad).

By extension, *dike* also refers to the entire process or system within which disputes were settled (here we follow Gagarin 1973, 89): "litigation process, legal system, law, rule of law" (9, 192, 213, 217, 220, 249, 256, 269, 275, 278, 279, 283). (*Dike* is personified at lines 220 and 256; in both cases we capitalize the noun.) Finally, *dike* can indicate a penalty as a result of the process (239); it is this meaning that informs the Athenian idiom *diken didonai,* "to give *dike,*" or "to pay a penalty."

In Homer, but not in Hesiod, *dike* may have a moral force and refer to proper or just behavior. In Hesiod, however, *dikaios* and *adikos,* the adjectives that are derived from *dike,* are grounded in this other, moral force; hence, we translate these adjectives "just" and "unjust."

Dike thus refers, in Hesiod, not so much to moral "justice" as to the process, in both its formal and its informal manifestations, of finding bearable solutions to disputes and of keeping the peace. The proceedings leading to *dike* as decision and traditional modes of dispute settlement in Asian villages may mirror each other sufficiently to illuminate the flexibility of *dike* in Hesiod's world. Village councils heard the "case." Just a few to all of the villagers could be present; anyone could present further evidence or argument and voice an opinion. Depending on the importance of the dispute and the numbers of people who felt strongly, such meetings could go on all day, even over several days. What ended the discussions was arrival at a consensus—not a *decision* about right or wrong, not a *vote* on the outcome, but a consensus that they had arrived at a decision with which they could all live. The consensus was accepted but not approved by all; some, even many, might have left the meeting despondent. It was a general agreement that no better solution could be found at the time. Certainly ideas about right and wrong affected the outcome, as did knowledge of relationships in the past, anticipation of the consequences of the terms of the settlement, the relative power of the participants, and the intensity of their feelings. In addition, the participants were not only the immediate parties to the dispute but everyone who chose to voice an opinion. The objective of such proceedings was to make it possible for everyone in the village to continue to live together and to carry on their functions. If a powerful man felt strongly, his views might shape the settlement; if he did not much care, a person with little power but who felt strongly could have appreciable influence on the outcome. (Even the most downtrodden had some power if they had allies—even other downtrodden—with whom everybody had to go on living.) The final articulation of the settlement was a summary by the village council of what had become obvious (with, perhaps, grunts of consent by the losing disputants).[19] In Indonesia this practice

19. These processes are common throughout South and Southeast Asia. Neale learned much about them while doing research in India (during 1955–56, 1960–61, and 1964–65), especially from people at the Institute of Community Development (Hyderabad), the Gokhale Institute of Politics and Economics (Poona), the Punjab Board of Economic Enquiry (Ludhiana), and the Planning, Research, and Action Institute (Lucknow). In conversa-

is called *gotong royong* (literally, the principle of harmony and its application to the settlement of disputes).

There are no clear lines between the immediate disputants and other interested parties; no clear lines between evidence and argument and opinion; nor is there a clear line between a "decision" and the emerging consensus. In all these respects the Asian village system resembles the *neikea* in the *agora.* Where the *basileus* alone gives *dike*—described by Hesiod in the *Theogony* as divinely inspired—his role appears similar to that of elders or council; and the fact that he gives *dike* after hearing all sorts of people speak, and after the opportunity to see the reactions of all present in the *agora,* certainly suggests that he is articulating an emerging consensus. Hesiod's description of this process and Homer's description of Achilles' Shield (see below, on *neikeu*) offer parallels to what we can observe in the Asian village.

This process is common in many small communities and may well be limited to small communities. It does not always work: witness the case of Achilles vs. Agamemnon, where two too-powerful people felt too intensely to allow a consensus to which they would subscribe. But note that the "case" then metamorphosed into something like the warriors vs. Agamemnon in the search for a solution—and this change was enough to get Agamemnon to subscribe to a consensus (although Achilles' consent

---

tions, scholars who have worked in Indonesia, the Philippines, and Thailand report the same thing. For summary statements, see Rosen 1975, 88–89, 101, 207. For accounts of how position (wealth, prestige, political power) affects the conduct and outcomes of disputes, see Bailey 1957, 104–6, 191–95, 203–5.

waited upon Patroclus's death, by which time the "case" had become the warriors vs. Achilles).

It is worth noting, furthermore, that Hesiod's confidence in the straight *dikai* of his leaders has been undermined somehow, that the *dikai* coming out from the *polis* to the countryside are becoming, in the opinion of those in the fields, more difficult to deal with and more threatening than before. This surely is an indication that the *polis,* at least in this part of Boeotia, is becoming more dominating (even as it becomes less welcome).

In North American society perhaps only families (and family-like groups) operate in this way (and children know what it is to be powerless in family discussions). The aim is the same: not that justice be done, but that all members of the group can continue to function within the group (see further Gagarin 1986, chap. 2).

Often one is especially interested in getting an advantageous *dike* when one is involved in a public dispute. We translate the Greek *neikos* (pl. *neikea*) "wrangling." When used in the context of the *agora*,[20] *neikos* approaches "lawsuit," meaning a publicly adjudicated dispute, a dispute brought into public space. There is the famous *neikos* on the Shield of Achilles, for example:

> The people were gathered in the *agora*. For there had arisen
> a wrangling (*neikos*), and two men were engaging in a wran-
> gling (*neikos*) over the payment for a man murdered. One
> claimed that he had paid in full, declaring as much to the

20. Wranglings often occur in the *agora,* which means "gathering place." It is not certain whether originally the *agora* was a gathering place for livestock or people; but it was becoming the new public space of the emergent *polis.* Since the term is still widely used, we do not translate it.

people (*demos*); the other refused to accept anything. Both were eager to receive the verdict from the knower [*istor;* see note 186]. The people were cheering both, supporting both sides. Heralds restrained the people, and there were old men sitting on polished stones within a sacred circle, and they were holding in their hands the staffs of the clear-voiced heralds. With these then they were darting up, and they were giving *dikai* each in turn. And in their midst there lay two talents of gold, to award to the man among them who might enunciate the straightest *dike*. (*Iliad* 18.497–508)

Here the two disputants each offer a *dike* (plea) as well as a stake of one talent (a large amount of metal). The judge who gives the straightest *dike* (best settlement) "wins" the stake. Presumably the onlookers judge which *dike* is best. It may not be "justice," but it keeps people from killing one another, no trivial accomplishment.

Perses appears to have had dealings or to be dealing with the *basilees* who enunciate *dikai* at Thespiae, dealings that have something to do with the fact that Perses has tried, is trying, or is about to try to get something from Hesiod that Hesiod does not want to give him. This action, coming, as it does, out of the *polis*, is also an example of what Hesiod thinks is wrong with the world. The system that allows the action appears to be the same as that which was responsible for Perses' own loss.

We close with a restatement of the limitations that we face in interpreting the poem. In addition to the lack of clarity that surrounds the starting point of the poem and the fuzziness of our understanding of the range of meanings of *dike*, problems arise from the structure of Hesiod's argument and from how one interprets the larger argument. Throughout, Hesiod complains about the bad *dikai* that are now being imposed on him and his neighbors, but what is bad about them is not clear. For instance, the *dike* that deprived Perses of his *oikos*—if that was what happened—was certainly bad for Perses; but it may have been reasonable, since, according to Hesiod, Perses "asked for it." The frequent statements to the effect that Zeus would not approve may be appeals to an "external, higher authority" representing a commonly accepted view of equity or justice. They may be resentful statements that these *dikai* are "not like the (good) ones we used to get." They may simply be inheritances from a splinter, "anti-aristocratic" branch of the oral tradition (Donlan 1973; Rose 1975; Farron 1979–80). There are other possibilities. We hypothesize that the "centers" of power used to have mutually supportive relations with farmers/peasants, but that the centers have recently withdrawn from their traditional and supportive redistributive role. If this be the case, then the appeals to Zeus may not refer to some commonly held idea of substantive justice but, rather, to an idea of proper procedures for arriving at *dike* (Gagarin 1973; 1974; 1986, 46–50; 1992). Then there is the possibility that Hesiod represented a newly literate but excluded class and was expressing opinions of its members: perhaps opinions that they had long held, perhaps opinions that were emerging along with the new social formations. Not necessarily inconsistent with this is the possibility that Hesiod may be appealing to an earlier, never-existing past, when things were, well, better.

WORKS AND DAYS

by Hesiod

1. *Pierian Muses.* Pieria is just north of Mt. Olympus in northern Greece. The Muses, the nine daughters of Zeus and Mnemosyne, "Memory," were born there (Hesiod tells this story at *Theogony* 53–62).

2. *Zeus.* Zeus is the chief god of the Greeks and leader of the Olympian gods. He is god of the bright sky and of the weather and in command (without question) of the array of gods and goddesses that inhabited the Greek world, many of whom Hesiod will speak of later.

How absolute or how tempered Zeus's power was is a difficult thing to decide. In oral poetry, inconsistencies are inevitable; it is no surprise then that Zeus is inconsistently portrayed in early Greek poetry. In the *Iliad* and *Odyssey,* Zeus's relationship to Fate can vary, just as his absolute authority over the other gods can be undermined in specific incidents. In *Works and Days,* Hesiod draws a consistent Zeus whose will is easily accomplished and illadvisedly resisted (see, for example, 105, 238–247).

In the *Theogony,* Hesiod tells us that Zeus's rise to heaven's throne is natural and opposed by none (389–403, esp. 402–403); Homer, on the other hand, states that the universe was divided up among Zeus, Poseidon, and Hades by the drawing of lots (*Iliad* 15.189–193). Lots were drawn to determine holders of leadership positions in many later Greek democracies; thus Homer's description introduces an egalitarian notion that is no doubt an expression of the new ideology of the incipient *polis.*

3. *dike.* See the Introduction, pp. 42–48.

4. *Strifes.* At *Theogony* 225f., Hesiod tells us that Night, the daughter of Chaos, bore "hard-hearted Strife," who is hated. He is correcting himself here, noting that there is also a good kind of

1   Pierian Muses,[1] who celebrate with songs, come here and tell of Zeus,[2] singing your father's praises; through him mortal men are equally unspoken and spoken, famed and unfamed by the aid of great Zeus. For easily he makes a man strong, but easily he presses hard the strong; easily he diminishes the illustrious and increases the unknown; easily he straightens the crooked man and withers the arrogant, does Zeus the High-Thunderer, who inhabits the loftiest homes. Heed with eyes and ears, and straighten decisions by means of *dike*.[3] I should like to speak the facts to Perses.

11   There was not only one race of Strifes,[4] but over the earth there are two. The one a man when he perceived her would praise; but the other is blameworthy. They have very

Strife; so there must be two of them. Eris is Strife's name in Greek. At the wedding of Peleus and Thetis (the parents of the warrior Achilles), Eris threw out a golden apple inscribed with the words "to the fairest," which precipitated an argument among the goddesses Aphrodite, Athena, and Hera. This led to the Judgment of Paris, which in turn led to the Trojan War. In mythology, then, Strife is no trivial goddess.

5. *evil war*. Throughout the translation "evil" represents the adjective *kakos*. There is a problem with this choice of word: in this instance and in most others, one should not read any condemnation into it; in this instance, for example, Hesiod is not passing judgment on war but, rather, observing the damage that it can cause.

6. *high-benched*. Zeus is imagined the helmsman of a boat, sitting on a higher bench than the oarsmen.

7. *Cronus*. Cronus is Zeus's father and was his predecessor as king in heaven, before the Titans were overthrown by the Olympians.

8. *oikos* (pl. *oikoi*). This word usually refers to an extended "household," more or less in the sense of the later Latin *familia*. That is, an *oikos* is a holding and everything on it: its production, structures, and residents. It also means "house" or "home."

9. *the good Strife . . . singer against singer*. Any economist would be struck by the similarity of this sentiment to economists' idea of "economic competition," including the fact that the activities of potters and carpenters are materially economic, while beggars compete for things and singers for employment.

10. *wranglings*. These are *neikea* (sing. *neikos*), discussed in the Introduction, pp. 46–47.

different spirits. The one supports evil war[5] and contention: she is cruel; no mortal is fond of her, but by necessity they honor the heavy Strife according to the plans of the deathless ones. The other gloomy Night bore first, and so the high-benched[6] son of Cronus,[7] who resides in the ether, placed her in the roots of the earth and made her much better for men. She rouses a man to work even if he is shiftless. For, if a person without work in hand sees another, a wealthy man who hurries to plow and plant and put his *oikos*[8] in good order, then that neighbor envies his neighbor who hurries after riches. This is the good Strife for mortals: potter is angry with potter and carpenter with carpenter; beggar bears a grudge against beggar, singer against singer.[9]

27   O Perses, put these things in your spirit. Do not let the evil-rejoicing Strife hold your spirit back from work while you closely watch wranglings[10] and play the listener

11. *agora.* See p. 46, esp. n. 20, in the Introduction.

12. *Demeter.* Demeter is the Olympian goddess of all crops, but especially of grains.

13. *support wranglings.* Supporting wranglings is what spectators did, rooting vociferously for their favorites, as on the Shield in the *Iliad* (see the Introduction, pp. 46 f.). Wranglings in the *agora* were apparently often over ownership or usufruct of land. Perses may have lost his holding (*kleros;* see note below) in a wrangling; now he may be trying to acquire Hesiod's in the *agora.* See pp. 39–48 in the Introduction.

14. *right here.* Temporal and locative: i.e., both straightway *and* away from the *agora.*

15. *holding.* This is *kleros. Kleros* is a holding or lot (same metaphor as our lot: piece of land / luck). One's *oikos* was situated on one's *kleros.* Here Hesiod apparently refers to the *kleros* that he and Perses inherited from their father. Note that the parental *oikos* was dissolved at the demise of their father and that it is the *kleros* that was subsequently divided between the two sons. Part of the problem that we witness here may be traced to the absence of primogeniture, which Hesiod will address later.

16. *energetically feeding the pride.* This renders the Greek *mega kudainon,* literally, "giving honor (*kudos*) in abundance," in an attempt to combine the related activities of flattery and bribery.

17. *gift-eating.* This epithet attached to the *basilees* is potentially ambiguous, for it would certainly have been the case that a group of people gave gifts to their *basileus* and that often these would have been edible; hence "gift-eating" is an appropriate modifier for the leader of any number of identifiable small-scale societies, including the ones described by Homer and Hesiod.

in the *agora*.[11] There is little interest in wranglings and *agora* activities for the man whose seasonal sustenance does not lie stored up in abundance indoors, what the earth bears, Demeter's[12] grain. When you have collected your fill of sustenance, then you might support wranglings[13] and contention over the possessions of others. You will never have a second chance to do these things: right here[14] let us settle our wrangling with straight *dikai*, which are from Zeus and best. For we had already distributed the holding,[15] but you snatched and carried off many other things, energetically feeding the pride[16] of gift-eating[17] *basilees*, who are willing

Homer does not employ this term, but he has Achilles address Agamemnon as *demoboros*, "devourer of the people" (*Iliad* 1.231), clearly in a pejorative sense. So also in Hesiod: "gift-eating" is potentially value free or neutral, but here (and later at lines 221 and 264) it is used pejoratively.

18. *who are willing to propose a* dike *in this case.* It is unlikely that we will ever understand exactly what happened in the dispute between Hesiod and Perses. On this specific phrase we follow Gagarin (1974, 108). The phrase may imply that some *basilees* have already given a *dike* favoring Perses. Compare Evelyn-White: "who love to judge such a case as this"; Verdenius: "who are used to pronouncing the kind of verdict as is known here"; West: "who see fit to make this their judgment." Gagarin also gives a review of the various interpretations of this thorny phrase (1974, 108 n. 13). Hesiod and Perses can have a *basileus* try to decide their case, or they can decide it themselves ("right here," above). Hesiod obviously thinks the settlement will work out better if accomplished without help from the *agora* (Gagarin 1992, 72).

19. *Fools, . . . mallow and asphodel.* Mallow (a common wild herb good mainly as a laxative) and asphodel (a barely edible root) are references to the unluxurious fare of the simple life, the point here being that it is better to have simple things earned by honest work than to enjoy luxuries gotten dishonestly. More complexly: "By 'half' Hesiod means a toilsome life in which a certain prosperity is achieved; the 'whole' is an utterly untroubled life such as gods enjoy, but which is fraught with danger for mortals" (Crotty 1982, 43).

to propose a *dike* in this case.[18] Fools, they do not know by
how much half is more than the whole, nor how great a
blessing there is in mallow and asphodel.[19]

 42 For the gods hid and kept sustenance from people.
For [before this time] you would easily accomplish even
in one single day so as to have enough even for a full year,
even if you were an idler. Quickly would you put away the

20. *steering oar up in the smoke.* Putting it over the hearth dries it and keeps it dry, providing protection against mildew and rot. This is our first reference to the reality of having to sell one's production away from home, there no longer being any such outlets at Thespiae. The seaman's steering oar has become an essential piece of farming equipment. Alternatively, the presence of the oar may be viewed more simply as emblematic of new (economic) opportunities that have arisen.

21. *oxen.* There are many references to *boes* (sing. *bous*) in this poem. With one exception we always translate *boes* "oxen," by which we mean castrated bulls; it is not certain that Hesiod always meant this, since the word in Homer can refer to any bovine, male or female, and Hesiod himself speaks at line 591 of a *bous* who is "not yet a mother" (the exception).

22. *chest.* This word is *phren* (sing.), more often *phrenes* (pl.), usually translated "brain" or "wits"; for a long time the word has been thought to mean "lung," in the plural "lungs" (see Onians 1951, 23–40), but in fact refers in singular or plural to the chest cavity (see now Burnett 1991, 275–76). Hence our choice of "chest." (At line 455, we translate "imagination," because it seems necessary.) The *thumos,* which is located in the *phrenes,* is a kind of control center for the emotions, and we translate it "spirit." Homeric heroes (and probably Homer's audience) were not aware of where ideation in fact takes place. In Homer (as in Hesiod), the *phrenes* are "the location where a person performs certain emotional, volitional, and intellectual functions" (Darcus 1979, 172). The use of *phrenes* resembles the use of *heart* in English for the seat of emotions. The word usually translated "life breath" is *psyche;* we also translate its single occurrence, a metaphorical use,

steering oar up in the smoke,[20] and the works of the oxen[21] and the work-enduring asses would disappear. But Zeus hid it, struck with anger in his chest[22] because

in *Works and Days* "life breath" (686). In Homer, and in Hesiod's *Theogony*, the *psyche* is the breath of life that leaves the body when death occurs; it is located in the head (Onians, 108–10).

23. *Prometheus.* Son of the Titan Iapetus, Prometheus is the chief benefactor of the human race. His name means "Before-Thinker."

24. *deceived.* A reference to an event narrated in the *Theogony*, in which Prometheus fooled Zeus into choosing the inferior of two plates offered for dinner. Zeus (whose wisdom is unlimited sometimes and certainly this time) pretended to be deceived so that he might have an excuse for punishing the human race:

> For when the gods and mortal men were working on a settle-
> ment at Mekone, even then [Prometheus] divided up a great
> ox and with concentrated spirit served it, deceiving the mind
> of Zeus. For him he had laid out flesh innards rich in fat in the
> hide after covering it with the ox's stomach; for the men in turn
> he arranged for a wily trick and laid out the ox's white bones
> after covering them in glistening fat. It was then that the fa-
> ther of gods and men said to him: "Son of Iapetus, conspic-
> uous among all leaders, my good man, how unfairly did you
> divide up the portions." So spoke Zeus with aggressiveness, who
> knows unfailing plans. In turn Prometheus of crooked counsel
> spoke to him, smiling quietly, and he did not forget his wily
> trick: "Zeus, most glorious and greatest of the gods who live
> forever, choose whichever of these that your spirit urges you
> to." He spoke with a trick in mind. Zeus, who knows unfail-
> ing plans, knew and did not fail to recognize the trick; he
> foresaw in his spirit bad things for mortal men which were go-
> ing to be brought to fulfillment. With both hands he picked
> up the white fat, he became angry around his chest, and anger
> entered his spirit, when he saw the white ox's bones for a wily
> trick. (*Theogony* 535–555)

Prometheus[23] of crooked counsel had deceived[24] him. For that very reason he contrived pernicious woes for people. He hid fire. In turn the mighty son of Iapetus stole it back for people, from Zeus the Planner, in a hollow fennel stalk, escaping the notice of Zeus who delights in the thunderbolt. Struck with anger, Zeus the Cloud-Gatherer said to him: "Son of Iapetus, who know how to contrive above all others, you rejoice that you have stolen fire and cheated me in my chest, a great disaster for you yourself and also for men in the future. In return for fire, I will give them an evil thing, in which they may all delight in spirit as they embrace their evil."

25. *Hephaestus.* Son of Zeus and Hera, Hephaestus is the lame (hamstrung) craftsman among the Olympians.

26. *Athena.* Daughter of Zeus and Metis (goddess of vigilance and cunning), Pallas Athena is among other things the goddess of the arts, especially those of women.

27. *Aphrodite.* Daughter of Zeus and Dione (an obscure goddess), Aphrodite oversees sexual activities.

28. *Hermes.* Son of Zeus and Maia (a daughter of Atlas), Hermes is messenger of the Olympians and god of thieves.

29. *Dog-Killer.* This is Argeiphontes, a regular epithet (common also in the *Iliad* and *Odyssey*) of Hermes, usually interpreted as "Slayer of Argos" in reference to Hermes' defeat of Argos, the hundred-eyed (noncanine) guardian of Io, the bovine love interest of Zeus (Ovid *Metamorphoses* 1.601–746). But such epithets ought to refer not to a single exploit of a god but to a routine activity. As god of thieves, Hermes would appropriately help thieves by ridding them of their primary obstacle, the guard dog. See more fully West, pp. 368–69.

30. *Craftsman.* This is Amphigyeeis, usually translated "Lame One," as if it meant "crooked on both sides." But it means "handy" (Verdenius), literally, "limbed on both sides."

31. *the goddess Graces and lady Persuasion; . . . the fair-haired Seasons.* The Graces (Charites), Persuasion (Peitho), and the Seasons (Horae) are companions or attendants of Aphrodite and appear to be doing her work for her here.

32. *breast.* This (the *stethe* [pl.]) is not conceptually different from the *phrenes.* But since it's a different word, we offer a different translation.

59   So he spoke, and the father of men and gods laughed
out loud. He ordered the renowned Hephaestus[25] to mix
earth with water as quickly as he could, and to put into it
human speech and strength, and to make a desirable, fair
appearance of a virgin like the deathless goddesses in face;
then he ordered Athena[26] to teach her her works, to weave
on the elegant loom. And golden Aphrodite[27] he ordered
to pour on her head charm and painful yearning and limb-
devouring cares. And he commanded Hermes,[28] the messenger Dog-Killer,[29] to put in her a dog's thinking and a deceitful character.

69   So he spoke, and they obeyed the lord Zeus, the
son of Cronus. Straightway the famous Craftsman[30] molded
out of earth something resembling a revered virgin, in accordance with the plans of the son of Cronus. The goddess
gleaming-eyed Athena girdled and adorned her; the goddess
Graces and lady Persuasion put golden necklaces on her skin;
around her the fair-haired Seasons[31] crowned her with spring
blooms: Pallas Athena fitted the entire adornment to her
skin. Then in her breast[32] the messenger Dog-Killer molded
lies and wheedling words, and a deceitful character, according to the plans of Zeus the Heavy-Thunderer. Then in her
the herald of the gods put a voice, and he named this woman

33. *Pandora.* Hesiod gives an etymology for the woman's name: all (*Pan-*) the gods gave her as a gift (*-dora*).

34. *bread-eating men.* In the *Odyssey* and in Hesiod, men are characteristically "bread eaters," in contradistinction to the gods, who eat ambrosia, not bread. If the Greek word here, *alphestes,* is not derived from *alphi,* "barley," then it comes from the verb *alphano,* "I earn, I acquire," which would lead to the meaning "achiever, industrious one."

35. *Epimetheus.* Epimetheus is Prometheus's brother, the "After-Thinker."

36. *groups.* This represents the Greek word *phula* (sing. *phulon*). *phulon* is usually translated "tribe," but that would be wrong for pre-*polis* Greece; Walter Donlan (1985, 297) argues that in Homer "*phula* specified small local groups, parts of a larger group of followers." The individuals within a *phulon* are known as "companions" (*hetairoi:* see below, note 54).

37. *Expectation.* That Hesiod does not tell us why Expectation (*elpis*) did not leave the jar has prompted spirited debate. Verdenius reviews the major interpretations and concludes tentatively that *elpis,* usually translated "hope," must here denote "expectation (of evil)."

38. *Aegis-Mover.* This is an epithet of Zeus, because when he shakes the aegis all things tremble. The aegis, usually worn by Athena (who received it as a gift from her father), is the skin of Amalthea, the goat who nurtured the baby Zeus with her breast and cornucopia. So grateful was the father of gods and men that he skinned her and made her into a constellation.

Pandora[33] because all those who have Olympian homes gave her as a gift: she was a disaster for bread-eating men.[34]

83   But when he had fully brought about the sheer, ineluctable ruse, the father dispatched the famous Dog-Killer, swift envoy of the gods, bearing the gift into Epimetheus's[35] home; and Epimetheus did not consider that Prometheus had told him never to accept a gift from Olympian Zeus, but to send it back again, lest somehow it turn out to be something evil for mortals. Then the receiver, just as he took hold of the evil, realized it.

90   For previously groups[36] of people lived on the ground, apart from and without evils and without hard toil and painful diseases, which give dooms to men. But the woman removed with her hands the jar's great lid and scattered the evils: she contrived pernicious woes for people. Expectation[37] alone remained there in her unbreakable home inside, under the jar's lips, and did not fly out, for Pandora had already thrown the jar's lid back on, according to the plans of Zeus the Aegis-Mover[38] and Cloud-Gatherer. Countless other pernicious things roam among people, for the earth is full of evils, and the sea is full. There are diseases for people during the day, and others in the night that wander under their own power, bringing evils to mortals secretly because Zeus the

39. *sprung from the same source.* Ordinarily this should refer to people and gods being descended from the same blood source. But here it must refer to the Golden Race, who "lived like gods" (112).

40. Lines 109–201. Hesiod drew the following tale of the degenerative races of humans from the Near East, apparently himself inserting the race of heroes between the Bronze Race and the Iron Race. There are parallels to be found throughout the Near East; perhaps the best known is the statue that appeared in Nebuchadnezzar's dream at Daniel 2.32–34. See West (1978, 172–77) for the pedigree of the tale. For subtle readings of the Hesiodic version, we recommend the provocative work of Jean-Pierre Vernant (1983a [1960], 1983b [1966]).

41. *unchanged in feet and hands.* That is, showing no signs of aging.

42. *excellent prize.* It is excellent (*basileios*) because it is the best one: the *basileus* always gets the first choice of prizes. This interpretation is supported by the Silver Race's second position (142). The prize, *geras,* is their power to give wealth. See further Donlan 1989, 131–32.

Planner took out their voice. Thus there is no way at all to avoid the purpose of Zeus.

106   If you see fit, I will tell you another story right to the end, well and skillfully. Toss it about in your chest, how gods and mortal people are sprung from the same source.[39]

109[40]   At the very first the deathless ones who have Olympian homes made a golden race of mortal people, who existed at the time of Cronus, when he was *basileus* in heaven. They lived like gods with woe-free spirit, apart from and without toils and grief; wretched old age did not hang over them, but unchanged in feet and hands,[41] they delighted in festivities beyond all evils. They died as if overcome by sleep. They had all good things. The grain-giving plowland of her own will bore her produce, much of it, and without grudging. And they enjoyed the fruits of their works in ease and peace with many good things, [*rich in sheep, dear to the blessed gods]. But ever since the earth covered over this race, they are divinities in accordance with the plans of great Zeus, and good ones on the ground, guardians of mortal people [*—they watch over *dikai* and cruel works, wrapped in mist, wandering everywhere over the earth], givers of wealth: and this is the excellent prize[42] that they got.

127   Later those who have Olympian homes in turn made a second race, much worse, from silver, resembling the

43. *violence.* This is our translation of *hubris. hubris* is a disregard for process, thus the precise antithesis of *dike* (clear in line 213 below), and "violence" seems the best rendering in this context.

44. *honor.* This is our translation of *kudos,* in Homer applied only to the living. An approximate synonym is *kleos,* "fame," which Homer uses also of the dead. *kudos* is what Perses dishes out when he feeds the pride of the *basilees* above in line 38.

45. *Meliae.* When Cronus castrated his father, Uranus, among those born from his blood and semen mixing with the Earth were the Giants and the Meliae, a group of nymphs here construed as the mothers of the Bronze Race. (Hesiod tells that story at *Theogony* 178–187.) *Melia* is an ash tree, from which Homeric spears are made.

46. *Ares.* Ares is the Greek god of warfare and violence.

47. *they did not eat bread at all.* Thus they stand in contrast to people today, who do eat bread (see above, line 82).

48. *adamant.* The Greeks had a wonderful notion of a resistless kind of iron that was supremely invincible (*a-damas*). It does not appear in Homer, perhaps because humans do not use it (or because heroes used bronze weapons). Here it is used metaphorically, as is the case also at *Theogony* 239.

golden one in neither physique nor thought. By contrast a child was nurtured playing at his devoted mother's side for a hundred years in his *oikos,* an utter fool. But precisely when [each] reached puberty and reached the peak of his youth, they lived for a very short time, having pains on account of their follies: for they were not able to hold back outrageous violence[43] from each other, and they did not see fit to serve the deathless ones, not even to do actions at the holy altars of the blessed ones, which is proper behavior for people according to their customs. These then Zeus, the son of Cronus, hid away in his anger, because they did not give honors to the blessed gods who hold Olympus. But ever since the earth covered over this race, these are called blessed mortals under the ground; they belong to the second rank, but honor[44] attends upon them all the same.

143   Father Zeus made another race, the third, of mortal people, from bronze, in no way like the silver one, born from the Meliae,[45] terrible and powerful. The moanful works of Ares[46] and acts of violence were their care; and they did not eat bread at all[47] but had a haughty spirit of adamant;[48] they were crude; great force and invincible hands grew from their shoulders on their sturdy limbs. Their weapons were made of bronze; their *oikoi* were made of bronze; they worked in bronze: there was no black iron. These, too, overcome by

49. *Aides.* This early form of the name Hades, the god of the Underworld, reveals the traditional Greek belief that his name meant "Unseen One" (A-ides).

50. *the race before ours over the immense earth.* Hesiod inserted this race in this place in the narrative either to acknowledge the "existence" of the Trojan War and other stories or to contradict the positions of those who claimed descent from the heroes, for, Hesiod tells us, the heroes all perished or were whisked away by Zeus: in effect, none of us can be descended from them.

51. *Thebe.* This is another name for Thebes, founded by Cadmus (162) and ruled famously by Oedipus (163). Hesiod tells us that two great events brought an end to the race of heroes, the battle at Thebes and the Trojan War a generation later, when the Greek heroes went to Troy to avenge the theft of Helen of Sparta by Paris.

one another's hands, went to the moldy house of icy Aïdes,[49] nameless. Black death took hold of them, impressive though they were, and they left behind the sun's bright light.

156 But when also this race the earth covered over, in turn Zeus, the son of Cronus, made another one, the fourth, on the much-nourishing ground, more just and so superior, a godly race of hero men, who are called demigods, the race before ours over the immense earth.[50] Evil war and the dreadful battle cry destroyed some of these below seven-gated Thebe,[51] the land of Cadmus, as they fought for the sheep of Oedipus. Others [perished] in their ships after war carried them over the great maw of the sea to Troy for fair-haired Helen's sake. There indeed the end of death covered some of them; to the rest father Zeus, the son of Cronus, offered sustenance and haunts apart from people and settled them at the boundaries of the earth. And these reside with woe-free spirit on the islands of the blessed ones on the shore of deep-eddying Ocean. They are prosperous heroes, for whom the grain-giving plowland bears honey-sweet produce thriving three times per year [*far from the deathless ones; Cronus is their *basileus*. For the father of men and gods set him free. Now among them ever since he has honor, as is seemly. Zeus then made another race of mortal men, from whom today's men are sprung over the much-nourishing land].

52. *grey-templed at birth.* This would be the logical extreme of the process implied by the 100-year childhood of the Silver Race: Iron Race people will be born old.

53. *resemble.* This denotes physical, not psychological, similarity (on account of marital fidelity).

54. *companion.* A companion (*hetairos*) is more than a friend (*philos*), either because of kinship or because of a swearing of allegiance. Free members of a powerful *oikos* were *hetairoi* to one another and to the leader of the *oikos*. A *phulon* (above, line 90 and note 36) was made up of *hetairoi*. Note how Odysseus's *hetairoi* share in a division after the adventure with the Cyclops:

> Now when we reached the island where the other well-benched ships lay moored together, our *hetairoi,* ever expecting us, sat weeping; then we got there and dragged our ship onto the sand, and from it we ourselves debarked onto the shore of the sea. We took the lambs of the Cyclops from the hollow ship and divided them up so that no one on my account might be cheated of an equal share. The ram my well-greaved *hetairoi* gave separately to me alone when the sheep were divided up. (*Odyssey* 9.543–551)

55. *vengeance of the gods.* Repeated refusal to perform appropriate actions, be they sacrificial or familial, will generate the gods' ill will.

56. *shame.* Shame is a sense of right and wrong; it is personified below at lines 200 and 324. *aidos* is a fear of shame that can prevent bad behavior and thus can be perceived as a great benefit. *aidos* is also the very shame that attends upon a person in the aftermath of bad behavior; it is this after-feeling that makes fear of shame effec-

174 Therefore, would that I were not now among the fifth [race of] men but had either died before them or been born afterwards. For now the race is indeed of iron. Not ever during the day will men cease from labor and grief; not even at night will they cease from being oppressed. The gods will give hard cares. And all the same, for even these, good things shall become mixed with evil things. And Zeus will destroy this race of mortal people too, when they turn out to be grey-templed at birth.[52] Father will not resemble[53] his children, and children in no way [will resemble father]; guest will not be friendly to host, companion[54] to companion and brother [to brother], as was the case before. They will quickly dishonor their parents as they grow old. Indeed, the cruel ones will find fault with them, addressing them with hard words, not reckoning at all with the vengeance of the gods;[55] and again they would not give to their aged parents in return for their upbringing. They will be men for whom *dike* is [strength of] hands: one man will sack another man's *polis*. There will be no goodwill for him who keeps his oath, not for the just, not for the good man, but men will sooner honor for his violence the man who is a doer of evils. *dike* will be in [strength of] hands, and shame[56] will not exist. The evil man will hurt the superior man by speaking with crooked words and will swear an oath on them. Envy, foul-

tive. The classic discussion of Greek shame is Dodds 1951, now superseded brilliantly by Bernard Williams (1993).

57. *group.* This is *phulon* again (see above, note 36).

58. *Nemesis.* Shame and Nemesis "are forces that inhibit wickedness, one working from inside, the other, public disapproval [Nemesis], from without" (West).

59. Lines 202–212. This fable, probably borrowed from the East, is challenging because Hesiod fails to explain why he introduced it, since in it the hawk (= *basilees*) bullies the nightingale (= Hesiod and his neighbors) without punishment. Modern sensibility, at least, expects there to be criticism of the hawk-*basileus,* but the absence of this appears to be more the result of a shortcoming of modern sensibility than of any shortcoming on the part of Hesiod. For a synopsis of the varying interpretations, see Lonsdale 1989. Thomas Hubbard's forthcoming work on this problem ingeniously suggests that the nightingale is Perses, who has erred by attempting to put himself on the same level as the local *basilees;* Hesiod thus urges Perses to know his place and to stay in it.

60. *singer.* The Greek word here is *aoidos,* the term in Homer for a composer of epic poetry.

61. *wretched. deilos* here refers to a social inferiority; "good" (*esthlos*) to the other end of the social spectrum.

mouthed, evil-rejoicing and ugly-faced, will accompany
all pitiful people. And just then to Olympus from the wide-
wayed ground, having covered their fair skin with white
robes, into the company of the group[57] of the deathless ones
will go Shame and Nemesis,[58] having left people behind.
Pernicious pains will be left behind for mortal people; there
will be no defense against evil.

202[59]   Now I will tell a fable to *basilees,* although they
themselves perceive it. Thus the hawk addressed the speckle-
necked nightingale, as he carried her very high in the clouds,
keeping her snatched in his talons. She was weeping pite-
ously, pierced by his curved talons, he addressed her haugh-
tily: "Strange one, why do you scream? Now one who is much
superior holds you. You will go wherever I myself carry you,
even though you may be a singer.[60] A meal I will make of you,
if I see fit, or I shall let you go. Foolish is he who sees fit to set
himself up against those who are better; he both loses the
victory and suffers pain in addition to disgrace." So spoke
the swift-winged hawk, the long-winged bird.

213   O Perses, listen to *Dike* and do not support
violence. For violence is evil for a wretched[61] mortal; not
even a good man can bear it easily, but he is weighed down
by it when he has met with calamities. By the other way
is the better road to [travel on and to] reach just things.

62. *dike.* Here *dike* is possibly but not certainly the "rule of law" (not certainly because straight *dikai* that prevent violence could be compromises). In the next sentence the *dikai* are clearly either pleas or judgments (or both).

63. *Oath.* This is another example of Hesiod's free use of personification. It is metaphoric rather than literal: Hesiod's world is not filled with these abstractions. We learn later (804) that Oath (Horkos) is a son of the bad Strife (Eris).

64. *And therefore they do not go onto ships.* This remark—which implies a strong distaste for the sea—becomes explicable later in the poem, when Hesiod discusses moving goods by sea.

dike[62] holds violence in check when it comes to the reckoning, asa fool realizes after suffering. For Oath[63] straightway chases down crooked *dikai,* and there is a clamor when *Dike* is dragged wherever gift-eating men carry her as they sort out decisions with crooked *dikai.* Wailing and wrapped in mist, *Dike* pursues the *polis* and the haunts of the people, bringing with her evil for people who would drive her out and who have dealt out *dike* that was not straight.

225   But those who give straight *dikai* to outsiders and insiders and do not diverge at all from what is just, for them the *polis* thrives, and the people in it bloom. And Peace, who nurtures children, is throughout the land; Zeus the Wide-Viewer never assigns painful war to them. And never do Hunger or Calamity attend upon men of straight *dikai,* but they enjoy at festivities the fruits of the works they have tended. For them the earth bears much sustenance, and in the mountains the oak bears acorns on top and bees in the middle. Their woolly sheep become heavy all over from their fleeces; women bear children that resemble their parents. They thrive with good things continually. And therefore they do not go onto ships,[64] but the grain-giving plowland bears [enough] produce [every year].

238   To those whose care is evil violence and cruel works Zeus the Wide-Viewer, the son of Cronus, assigns *dike.*

65. *thirty thousand.* Hesiod says thrice ten thousand, ten thousand being the largest number in the Greek poetic vocabulary; its use here and elsewhere in early poetry is analogous to the modern use of "million" or perhaps "billion."

66. *virgin.* The Greek word is *parthenos,* and so Hesiod makes reference to pure and uncorrupted justice. Alternatively, one may wish to take *parthenos* as "unmarried," in which case the (legal) point here would be that she has no husband to speak up for her (hence her rape above: "there is a clamor when *Dike* is dragged . . ."); having no husband then, she goes to the side of Zeus, her father, who takes care of things on her behalf.

67. *people.* This is our rendering of the collective singular noun *demos,* which refers to both the population of a place and the territory that the population occupies. At times the *demos* includes all people, at other times only those not situated in the political center, clearly the case here. This is the earliest use of the term to indicate tension between center and *demos.* For a full discussion of *demos* in early poetry, see Donlan 1970, 383–85.

In our translation up to this point, and hereafter, "people" has been a rendering of *anthropoi,* "human beings," and occasionally also of *laoi,* a collective term for people. "Man" or "men" renders the Greek word *aner* (pl. *andres*).

Many times even the entire *polis* fares ill for an evil man who commits offenses and plots actions of outrage. On them the son of Cronus brings a great disaster from heaven: hunger and plague together. The people die; women do not give birth; *oikoi* become diminished by the ploys of Olympian Zeus. At different times in turn the son of Cronus destroys their wide army, or their wall, or exacts atonement from their ships upon the open sea.

248 O *basilees*, you too observe well this *dike*, for the deathless ones, who are near among people, observe all those who wear each other out with crooked *dikai*, paying no attention to the vengeance of the gods. For there are over the much-nourishing ground thirty thousand[65] deathless guardians of mortal people, sent from Zeus; they watch for *dikai* and cruel works, wrapped in mist, wandering everywhere over the earth. And there is the virgin[66] *Dike,* born from Zeus, majestic and revered among the gods who hold Olympus. And whenever somebody hurts her by scorning her crookedly, she straightway seats herself at the side of father Zeus, the son of Cronus, and tells him about the unjust thinking of people, until the people[67] atone for the outrages of the *basilees* who, by thinking pernicious thoughts, veer off the right track by pronouncing *dikai* crookedly.

263 Watching for these things, O *basilees,* straighten

68. dike *this is.* This is the same locution that Hesiod uses in line 39, when he refers to his own legal wrangling with his brother and the *basilees* "who are willing to propose a *dike* in this case." It is difficult to argue that Hesiod wishes us to see the similarity of diction, but we point it out nevertheless. The *dike* earlier referred to a specific judgment; here it refers to the system generally.

69. *argue.* Implicit in this is a public action in the *agora.*

70. *failure. kakotes* is the noun form from the adjective *kakos,* which is translated "evil" (see note 177). Here it is the social obverse of *arete* (see note 71).

your words, gift-eaters, and forget entirely crooked *dikai*. The man who constructs evils for another constructs evils for himself, and the evil plan is most evil for the one who has planned it. The eye of Zeus that has seen all and perceived all even now looks, if he has seen fit, on these things, and it does not escape his notice just what kind of *dike* this is[68] that the *polis* contains within it.

270 Now indeed may I myself not be just among people, nor may my son, since it is an evil thing to be a just man, if the more unjust man will have greater *dike*. But I anticipate that Zeus the Planner will never bring these things about.

274 O Perses, toss these things behind your chest and listen now to *Dike*. Forget about force completely. For this usage did the son of Cronus grant to people: fishes and land animals and winged birds eat each other because *dike* is not in them. But to people he gave *dike*, which is by much the best thing: if someone sees fit to argue[69] just points knowingly, to him Zeus the Wide-Viewer gives prosperity; but whoever purposely lies by swearing a false oath at witness bearings and hurts *Dike* and is incurably infatuated, that man's family is left thereafter more obscure. The family of a man who keeps his oath is thereafter better.

286 Since I perceive good things, I will tell them to you, Perses, you utter fool. It is easy to seize failure[70] and in quan-

71. *success.* This is *arete,* whose usual translation is "excellence." In the epics, a hero strove to be recognized for his *arete;* here, in such a material economic context, it must be the same as *olbos,* "prosperity."

72. *That man is . . . of all things himself.* A typical (archetypical even) peasant sentiment: there is no more successful autarky than the absolute independence of an individual *oikos.*

73. *Hunger.* Here personified, Hunger is the son of the bad Eris (*Theogony* 226–227).

tities; the road is smooth: she resides very near. But before success[71] the deathless gods put sweat: long and straight up is the path to her and tough at first. When a man reaches the top, then indeed it is easy, though it was hard before.

293   That man is altogether the best who thinks of all things himself,[72] who has considered what is to come, how it may be better in the end. That man moreover is good who trusts a man who speaks well. But he who neither thinks himself nor listens to another when he tosses things about in his spirit, he is a man of no use.

298   But you, ever mindful of our bidding, get to work, Perses, glorious offspring, in order that Hunger[73] may detest you, and revered, goodly crowned Demeter may be fond of you and fill your granary with sustenance. For Hunger is an entirely natural companion for a man who is an idler; gods and also men resent him who lives as an idler, in temperament like the stingless drones who wear away the labor of the bees by eating, idlers that they are. Let it be important to you to keep your own works properly organized so that your granaries may become full of seasonal sustenance. It is from works that men are many-sheeped and rich, and the man who works is much dearer to the deathless ones. [*He will be to mortals also; for they especially hate idlers.] Work is no reproach: idleness is a reproach. If you work, the idler will

74. *injures and benefits men.* This is an excellent articulation of the ambiguity of *aidos* (see above, notes 56 and 58).

75. *poverty.* Here "poverty" is *anolbie,* literally, "unprosperity." Elsewhere "poverty" renders the word *penie,* which denotes the undesirable condition under which one person is required to work for another.

76. *kerdos* (pl. *kerdea*). "Advantage (for oneself)," as opposed to "advantage (for another)," which is rendered by *ophelos* in Homer. See further de Jong 1987, and the Introduction, pp. 36–37.

77. *prosperity attends him for a short time.* To this sentiment compare the Egyptian *Instructions of Amenemope* 9.10–19, esp. 16–17: "If riches come to you by theft, They will not spend the night with you" (Lichtheim 1976, 152).

78. *against what is proper.* This is a reference to the Greek principle of moderation, the avoidance of excess in all things, what Athenians later would call *sophrosyne.* See further note 172 below.

This section offers excellent examples of the strong language regarding appropriate community behavior that one finds time and again in the ethnographies of small-scale societies. This series of injunctions is both practical and moral, and in their own way they have much to do with *dike.*

quickly envy you as you become wealthy. Success and re-
nown attend upon wealth.

314   So whatever your situation may be, to work is the
advisable course, if by turning your witless spirit to work,
away from others' possessions, you give care to your livelihood, as I exhort you. Shame is not good at looking after the
needy man, shame which greatly injures and benefits men;[74]
shame sits next to poverty,[75] confidence next to prosperity.
Goods are not for snatching; god-given things are much better. For if someone seizes great prosperity even by force with
hands, or carries it off with his tongue, as many times hap-
pens whenever *kerdos*[76] deceives the thinking of people, and
Shamelessness chases away Shame, then easily the gods make
him obscure, and they diminish that man's *oikos,* and prosperity attends him for a short time.[77] Likewise with him who
mistreats a suppliant or with him who mistreats a guest, and
with him who might climb into his brother's bed for the se-
cret bed-pleasures of his wife, acting against what is proper,[78]
and with him who offends on account of his follies against
somebody's fatherless children, and with him who raises a
wrangling with his old father at the evil threshold of old
age, assailing him with hard words. With that man Zeus
himself indeed is indignant, and so in the end in return for

79. *At other times . . . another man yours.* This sentence reminds us of Perses' specific problem: he lost his *kleros.* It also is an explicit statement about the alienability of land. Nowhere else does Hesiod encourage his brother to get someone else's *oikos,* only that he get an *oikos,* period. All things being equal, however, it is better to be in a position to acquire someone else's property rather than the other way around. Of course, when all *kleroi* are held, acquiring one necessarily involves separating it from someone else.

80. *feast.* This (and later) is a translation of *dais,* which is, literally, the "activity of dividing up" for sharing. These were clearly important events for the coherence of community. The *dais* in epic is an important context for the distribution and maintenance of power among the elite.

81. *neighbors come ungirt, while in-laws gird themselves.* That is, neighbors value one another so highly that they come to one another's aid immediately. Thus we see an explicit statement about the new importance of neighborly relations as opposed to kinship ones.

82. *become lost.* An ox would not become lost either by death or by disappearance. The Greek is ambiguous, but the sentiment is clear.

83. *pay it back well.* We must keep in mind the different rules that often govern (economic) behavior in primitive communities: "The premium set on generosity is so great when measured in terms of social prestige as to make any other behavior than that of self-forgetfulness simply not pay" (Polanyi 1944, 46). See further the Introduction.

unjust works he sets down hard requital. But keep your witless spirit completely away from these things.

336   As much as you can, do holy rites for the deathless
gods with purity and cleanliness, and burn splendid thigh-
bones on [the altars]. At other times propitiate with liba-
tions and burnt sacrifices, both whenever you go to bed and
whenever the holy light comes, so that the gods may have a
propitious heart and spirit toward you, so that you may acquire the holding of other men, and not another man yours.[79]

342   Call your friend to a feast,[80] but leave your enemy
alone. Call especially him who resides near you. For if a
problem arises at your place, neighbors come ungirt, while
in-laws gird themselves.[81] A bad neighbor is a disaster as
much as a good neighbor is a great blessing. He has his share
of honor who has a good neighbor. And an ox would not
become lost[82] unless your neighbor should be bad. Take
good measure from a neighbor, and pay it back well,[83] with
the same measure, or better if you can, so that you may later
find him reliable should you need him. Do not pursue evil
kerdea. Evil *kerdea* are the same as calamities.

353   Stay friendly to your friend; spend time with him
who calls on you; give to him who gives, and do not give
to him who does not give. One gives to a giver, but one
does not give to a nongiver. Give is good, but Snatch is evil,

84. *freezes his victim's poor heart.* The Greek is ambiguous as to whose heart is frozen in this action, the victim's or the perpetrator's. We suspect the former's is the more likely.

85. *Let the wage . . . equally destroy men.* Verdenius believes that these lines are genuine (they were first deemed a later addition by Wilamowitz [1928 ad loc.], followed by Solmsen and West); we agree that they fit into the broader picture as well as the specific situation between Hesiod and Perses. They fit generally, even if kin relations are no longer dependable; and they also fit specifically, if Hesiod apparently had no witness to whatever it is that he claims is the truth.

86. *fancy-assed woman.* Verdenius suggests that this refers to one's wife, since Hesiod will turn next to sons, but Renehan (1980, 353) makes it clear that this refers to a woman "seeking not necessarily marriage (nor money which did not exist) but one's (material) substance."

87. *another son.* This apparent contradiction to the injunction to have only one son has been dealt with variously. Among recent suggestions: "another son" refers to the next generation, that is, to a grandson (West ad loc.); most scholars (e.g., Renehan 1980, 353) choose to read this as a Hesiodic reference to his own situation, in which his father died young, not having provided sufficiently for two heirs. Richardson (1979, 170) suggests that Hesiod means that if the father is older, then the sons will be more mature and so will not argue. Karl Polanyi (1977, 152) offers another twist: "Life is still possible if there are two sons; but only if the father manages to grow old. In that case, the advantages of division of labor may outweigh the burden of the fragmentation of the land through inheritance." Of course, there may not be any contradiction at all,

a giver of death. For he who gives willingly, even when he gives something great, rejoices in the giving and delights in his own spirit. But he who himself seizes, after trusting in shamelessness, even if it be something little, freezes his victim's poor heart.[84]

361 For if you should put away a little on top of a little, and you should do this often, quickly even that little would become big. He who adds to what is there wards off blazing hunger. What lies stored up in his *oikos* does not wear down a man: it is better in the *oikos,* since what is outside is at risk. It is good to take hold of what is at hand; it is a disaster to the spirit to need what is absent. I command you to consider these things.

368 Take your fill when the jar is at its start and at its finish. Be sparing in the middle; sparing is worthless in the lees. [*Let the wage promised to a man who is a friend be reliable; and as you laugh with your brother put up a witness, for indeed trustings and mistrustings equally destroy men.][85] Do not let a fancy-assed woman[86] deceive you in your thinking by chattering wheedling words while she keeps an eye on your granary. He who trusts a woman trusts thieves. May there be an only son to feed his father's *oikos,* for thus wealth increases in the halls; may you die an old man, if you leave behind another son.[87] Easily would Zeus

if all Hesiod is doing is referring to the common failure to limit the family size to the ideal size. Bailey (1957, 90–91) observes that in Bisipara, an Indian village in highland Orissa, landholdings tended to accrue to families where a succession of single males enjoyed the family inheritance; landholdings were typically lost where there was a succession of multiple sons.

88. *pile work upon work upon work.* This is an attempt to render the Greek, which literally says "work (imperative verb) work (object) upon work (prepositional phrase)."

89. *Pleiades.* The Pleiades are a group of stars in the constellation Taurus. They appear to have a role in the weather as it is pertinent to agricultural timeliness (here, 572, 615: *pleion* is a Greek word for "seed") and also to sailing (619: *plein* means "to sail"). They are setting in early November and are rising in May, after being out of sight for about forty nights; planting in November and reaping in May must mean Hesiod is talking about winter wheat. The Greek folk-etymology is that these daughters of Atlas are "Doves."

90. *Atlas.* Atlas holds up the heavens as penalty for fighting on the losing side in the battle between the Titans and the Olympians; he is a brother of Prometheus.

91. *iron is being sharpened.* This is a reference to sharpening the sickles for reaping (cf. line 573 below), not a reference to an iron plowshare.

give unquenchable prosperity to more persons. The care of more hands is more, and the increase is greater. If the spirit in your chest desires wealth, do these things, and pile work upon work upon work.[88]

383   When the Pleiades,[89] the daughters of Atlas,[90] are rising, start the reaping; start the plowing when they are setting. Indeed they lie hidden for forty nights and days, and when the year has gone round they first appear again when the iron is being sharpened.[91] This is the usage of the plains, of both those who reside near the sea and those who inhabit the hollows in the glens, the fat place far from the swelling open sea: sow stripped, work your oxen stripped, and reap stripped, if you see fit to give heed to all of Demeter's works in their season, in order that they may each increase in their season, and lest, perhaps by gaping after things behind you, you go begging at others' *oikoi* and effect nothing.

396   Thus even now you came to me; but I will not give you anything more nor will I measure out anything further. Perses, you fool, work the works that the gods have assigned to people, lest at some time with your children and wife and with an ache in your spirit you may seek sustenance among your neighbors, and they do not care. For twice, perhaps three times, you will get results. But if you vex them further, you will not achieve a thing; you will make many vain argu-

92. *chrea. chrea* are debts of a new type; see pp. 39–42 in the Introduction.

93. *a bought woman . . . oxen.* There has been some lively debate over whether this line belongs here. Aristotle twice quotes the previous line intending the "woman" there to mean wife, which of course is precisely contrary to the point of the following line. West cannot decide, pointing out that all "help on the land is provided by men." In India women (and children) may follow the oxen to pick up the dung, which is used for plastering, fuel, and fertilizer.

94. *autumn.* The rains begin in September.

95. *skin . . . much more comfortable.* One's complexion improves.

96. *Sirius.* The daytime rising of Sirius, the Dog Star, marked the hottest day of the year for the Greeks, about July 19. It is September now, and Sirius is overhead more during the night than during the day.

97. *Then.* The period referred to is after July 19.

98. *three-foot.* A Greek foot was between 11½ and 13 inches.

99. *three-cubit.* One cubit equaled 1½ feet.

100. *mortar, . . . pestle.* Every farm needed a heavy-duty mortar and pestle for grinding wheat or any other material that was unsuitable for the millstone because of volume or shape. This mortar is 3 feet high, just right for the standing pestler, whose 4½-foot instrument's potential unwieldiness would be reduced by tapering it at the middle (at the grip).

ments, and your repertoire of words will be of no use. I command you to consider discharge of *chrea*[92] and avoidance of
hunger.

405 First of all [get yourself] an *oikos* and a woman
and a plower ox—a bought woman, not a wife, one who
could follow the oxen[93] and get all goods into their right
place in the *oikos,* lest you need to ask another who refuses
and then you are short, while time goes by and your work
becomes diminished. Do not put off work until tomorrow
or the day after tomorrow. For the man who works at vain
tasks does not fill his granary, nor does the man who puts
things off. Care supports work; the man who puts off work
is always wrestling with calamities.

414 Just when the might of the sweat-causing heat of the
keen sun ceases, and Zeus the Strong has sent the autumn[94]
rains, then does a man's skin change to become much more
comfortable.[95] For at just that time the star Sirius[96] goes
over the head of born-for-doom people for a little while during the day but has a larger share of the night.

420 Then[97] is wood least worm-eaten when cut with the
iron: it drops its leaves to the ground and ceases from sprout-
ing. Precisely then, remember to cut wood, the work of that
season. Cut a three-foot[98] mortar, then a three-cubit[99] pestle,[100]

101. *seven-foot axle.* West thinks that a seven-foot axle is too long for this wagon, that the wagon would be too wide to work right, but Piggott (Richardson and Piggott 1982, 228) makes clear that this size of axle would generate a wheel gauge of about 1.3 meters, precisely in keeping with the wheel gauges of buried eighth-century chariots and with the ruts left in ancient roads.

102. *mallet.* A mallet is handy for breaking up the harder clods.

103. *three-span.* Three spans make 2¼ feet.

104. *felloe.* The felloe is the outside rim of a wheel. Here the term must indicate (as it does elsewhere in ancient Greece) a quarter-felloe, four of which when fitted together make up the wheel's rim, which would have a circumference of 9 feet (and diameter of 2½ to 3 feet).

105. *ten-quarter-foot wagon.* For this description to continue to make sense, one needs to assume that this measurement of 2½ feet refers not to the wagon's height, length, or width, but to the diameter of the wagon's wheels—more precisely, the length together of the two spokes that run between axle and felloes.

106. *many timbers bent at an angle.* This refers, of course, to the importance of choosing the right woods for your goals. Already bent materials were preferred to straight pieces that would require more shaping. It is reasonable to presume that the necessary woods were collected by farmers according to size and type, to be delivered later to specialist builders of wagons and plows, just as it is likely that farmers brought iron and other metals to smiths to make into whatever the farmers needed.

107. *plow tree.* The plow tree (*gues*) is the part of the plow extending upward from the plow stock. See figure 3.

and a seven-foot axle:[101] thus it would fit right for you.
With eight feet, you might also cut a mallet[102] head from it.
Cut a three-span[103] felloe[104] for a ten-quarter-foot wagon;[105]
[cut] many timbers bent at an angle.[106] Carry into your *oikos*
a plow tree[107] made from holm oak, whenever you find
one as you search through the mountain and through the
plowland. This one is stoutest to plow with with oxen, when

108. *slave of Athena.* A slave of Athena would be a carpenter, significant because there is the implication of specialist labor, with such specialists moving from *oikos* to *oikos*.

109. *plow stock.* The plow stock (*eluma*) is the part that turns the earth, to which an iron plowshare would be attached if one was used.

110. *yoke pole.* The yoke pole (*histoboeus*) connects the plow tree to the yoke.

111. *naturally.* That is, with a single piece of wood serving as *gues* and *eluma*. Why Hesiod suggests one "natural" and one "fitted" is puzzling.

112. *nine-year-old male oxen.* This apparent redundancy (oxen are by definition male) reflects the possible but not usual range in meaning for the Greek word *bous* (see note 21). Nine seems a late age to speak of prime strength, if we are able to compare arrangements in India, where oxen start work at age three, weakness of old age being expected at age twelve to fourteen. More important than strength, however, is discipline: the first few years of an ox's working career are less productive than later ones because the ox has not learned his routines yet. By eight or nine years old, an ox will turn himself at the end of the plow row.

113. *crane.* Cranes migrate in October and November.

a slave of Athena[108] has fixed it to the plow stock[109] with dowels and has brought it and fitted it to the yoke pole.[110] Make two plows by toiling away inside your *oikos,* one with the plow tree formed naturally,[111] one fitted together; this is the advisable course. If you should break one, you would throw the other on your oxen. Yoke poles made from laurel or elm are most worm-free; likewise the plow stock made from oak, the plow tree from holm oak.

436   Take possession of two nine-year-old male oxen,[112] for their strength is not easily spent who are at the peak of their youth; two such are best for working. They would not quarrel in the furrow and so break a plow and straight way leave your work in vain. Let a forty-year-old fellow follow along with them, after eating from a loaf broken into four but designed to be in eighths; that one, caring for his work, would drive a straight furrow, no longer gaping after those his own age, but keeping his spirit on his work. And no younger man is any better at distributing seeds and avoiding oversowing than he. For a man who has more lad in him is aroused among those his own age.

448   Consider, whenever you hear the voice of the crane[113] screeching out her yearly cries from on high out of the clouds: she brings the signal of plowing and points out the time of rainy winter; she stings an oxless man's heart. At just

114. *plowing* [*time*]. This is the time for the fall planting of the winter wheat, when the Pleiades are rising, and the cranes are migrating.

that time feed fodder to the twisted-horned oxen that are indoors.

453 It is rather easy to say the words: "Give me two oxen and a wagon"; but it is as easy to reject the idea: "There are works for my oxen." A man rich in imagination boasts that he will build a wagon, but that fool does not know this: there are a hundred timbers to a wagon. Have the care to put them up in your *oikos* beforehand.

458 When at the very first the plowing[time][114] appears

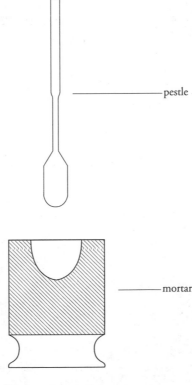

Figure 1.

115. *soother of children.* This is the traditional interpretation of the transmitted text; West objects and alters the text to read "soother of Aïdoneus" (another name for Hades). This is also how he renders the half-line in his translation (West 1988). The transmitted reading is probably superior; see Marquardt 1984. The fallow field is a soother of children because it is part of a broad system of production that has an eye for the future.

116. *Zeus In-The-Ground.* This is Hades euphemistically. Hades, mentioned in line 153 by the name Aïdes, is the brother of Zeus and ruler of the dead in the Underworld. He is linked here, as often, with Demeter, because he was treated by the Greeks as not just a taker, but also a giver of life, often called the "wealthy one." Hence he is appropriately married to Demeter's daughter Persephone.

117. *plow tail.* The plow tail (*echetle*) is the handle; see figure 3.

to mortals, at just that time set out, equally both slaves and yourself, to plow at plowing time both wet and dry [land], hurrying especially at daybreak, in order that your plowlands may become full. Turn up [the soil] in the spring; in the summer a once-plowed [fallow] field will not deceive you. Sow a fallow plowland when the ground is still light. A fallow field is a protector against ruin and a soother of children.[115]

465   Pray to Zeus In-The-Ground[116] and pure Demeter that Demeter's ripe holy grain may become heavy, as at first you start the plowing, whenever you take the top of the plow tail[117] with your hand and come down with your switch

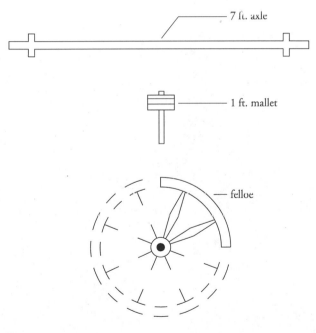

7 ft. axle

1 ft. mallet

felloe

Figure 2.

118. *yoke peg . . . yoke strap.* The yoke peg is where the plow was attached by the yoke pole (*histoboeus*) to the yoke. The yoke strap was tied around the juncture of yoke and plow and was the initial point of pressure when the oxen began their forward motion, as here.

119. *Olympian.* This is Zeus.

on the back of your oxen as they pull the yoke peg by the
yoke strap.[118] A little behind have a slave with a mattock
make toil for the birds by hiding the seed. For good organization is the best thing for mortal people; bad organization is
the worst.

473 Thus would the ears of grain nod to the ground vig-
orously, if the Olympian[119] himself should offer a good outcome thereafter; and you would sweep spiderwebs from your
vats; and I anticipate that you will be cheered as you take
hold of your substance that is indoors. You will reach bright

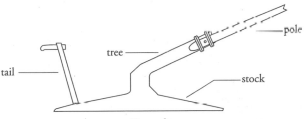

Natural

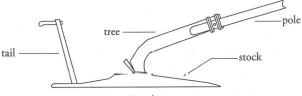

Fitted

Figure 3.

120. *turnings of the sun.* This is a reference to the solstice (here summer). See also below at line 564 (winter) and at line 663 (summer again).

121. *reap seated.* When the wheat is tall, it is cut in the middle; when it is short, near the ground the worker cuts it squatting on his heels.

122. *plow late.* To plow late would be to plow later than November, long after the Pleiades have risen, with not a crane to be heard anywhere.

123. *short of it.* We cannot improve on West: "I suppose this means that the puddles or mud that the oxen and cows walk through come up to the top of their hooves; or that hoofprints they have left in the soil fill with water without larger puddles appearing."

124. *Under these conditions . . . the early plower.* This appears to be an attempt to explain that late starters may still have a chance to succeed with their late plantings.

125. *talk-hall.* The talk-hall (*lesche*) appears to be a place where leisure time is spent away from the affairs of the *polis*. In a very late *Life,* Homer is said to have traveled to Cume and Phocaea to sing at the *lesche* of old men at each place. It is not a place of elegance, according to Penelope's opinion (she addresses the disguised Odysseus): "Wretched stranger, you are but someone touched in the head; you are unwilling to go to a smithy's place to sleep, or to some *lesche*" (*Odyssey* 18.327–329). Although sometimes the later *leschai* are associated with communal eating and drinking, "it is clear that the activities generally regarded as characteristic of the *lesche* differ from those associated with banquets

spring in good shape and will not gaze at others: another man shall be in need of you.

479   If you plow the glorious ground at the turnings of the sun,[120] you will reap seated,[121] grasping a little bit in your hand, tying together the sheaves head to foot, covered in dust, not overly rejoicing, and you will carry it off in a basket. Few men will look at you with admiration.

483   The purpose of Zeus the Aegis-Mover is different at different times and is painful for mortal men to perceive. If you plow late,[122] this would be your remedy: when the cuckoo first cuckoos in the leaves of the oak and delights mortals over the immense earth, then Zeus may send rain on the third day and he may not cease, neither exceeding the hoof of an ox nor falling short of it.[123] Under these conditions the late plower might compete with the early plower.[124] Watch out well for all this in your spirit, and let neither bright spring's arrival nor the rain in its season escape your notice.

493   Pass by the smithy's seat and the warm talk-hall[125] in wintertime, when the cold keeps men back from their works. At that time a diligent man would support his *oikos* greatly, lest in the course of a bad winter Helplessness over-

and *symposia.* The essential ingredient was, not eating and drinking, but talk" (Buxton 1994, 41–42).

126. *Helplessness . . . along with Poverty.* In early Greek Poetry, Helplessness and Poverty are often paired and regularly closely related: "Poverty who brings down a great people with her sister Helplessness" (Alcaeus 364); "Poverty, the mother of Helplessness" (Theognis 384–385).

127. *swollen foot with a shriveled hand.* These are caused by malnutrition.

128. *huts.* This is the same word elsewhere translated "granary," and perhaps we should translate "build granaries" here. But the Greek verb requires a building of special concern for the addressees. During summer the men sleep outside; come winter that is impractical.

129. *Lenaion.* This is not a Boeotian month, but an Ionian month (meaning it was used by Athens, many of the central Aegean islands, and the cities of Ionia, which comprised roughly the southern half of the west coast of Asia Minor), which suggests that this is either a later addition or an indication of an attempt by Hesiod to reach a larger audience. Lenaion was a winter month (sometime between December's solstice and March's equinox) on the island of Delos and at Miletus in Ionia.

130. *ox-skinning.* We follow West: "The days are simply cold and windy enough to take the hide off an ox" (see his complete note for comparative information).

131. *Boreas.* This is the name of the north wind.

132. *Thrace.* Thrace is the land north of Greece, proverbially cold.

take you along with Poverty,[126] and you squeeze a swollen foot with a shriveled hand.[127] An idler, waiting for an empty hope and in need of sustenance, meditates on many evils in his spirit. Hope is not good at looking after a needy man who is seated in the talk-hall, whose sustenance is not sufficient. Explain to the slaves when the summer is still in its middle: "It will not always be summer: make yourselves huts."[128]

504   The month Lenaion[129]—bad days, all ox-skinning[130] days—avoid it and the hoarfrosts that become ruthless when Boreas[131] has blown over the earth, Boreas who blows through horse-nurturing Thrace[132] onto the wide open sea and stirs it up; the earth and the woods bellow. Falling upon many high-leaved oaks and thick pines in the glens of the mountain, Boreas brings them down to the much-nurturing ground, and then all the enormous woods shouts. Animals bristle, and they put their tails under their genitals, even those whose hide is covered with fur. Because Boreas is ice-cold he blows through them, even though they are shaggy-breasted. He goes through the hide of an ox, and it does not keep him out; he blows through the thin-haired goat. The power of the wind Boreas does not blow through the flocks [of sheep] at all, because their hairs are abundant; but he

133. *makes an old man into a wheel.* He does so by bending him over into a near-circular bow.

134. *Boneless One.* Traditionally this has been interpreted as a kenning or riddle for "octopus." See West for other suggestions (including a dinnerless sheepdog); more recently: "an invertebrate belonging to the phylum Coelenterata, and in all probability to the Class Scyphozoa" (Phillips 1980, 154). Calvert Watkins (1978) suggests that the Boneless One is the penis: in the winter Boreas cannot pierce the skin of virgins, who do not have knowledge of Aphrodite; therefore winter is the season when the penis sits idle. Just as passion eats at the lover's marrow in Old Irish, Sanskrit, and Anglo-Saxon, so does the penis metaphorically gnaw at itself when forced into inactivity.

It is very difficult to evaluate Watkins's suggestion. If he is right that Hesiod has without reflection inherited a very old Indo-European tradition, it nevertheless seems clear that Hesiod almost certainly does not know that he means penis; if Hesiod does not know that he means penis, it is hard to imagine what his audience thought this riddle may have been about.

135. *territory.* This also is *demos* (see note 67).

136. *the Dark Men.* This is a reference to Africans. Hesiod elsewhere groups together Undergrounders (a reference to their southernness), Pygmies, Black Men, and Ethiopians (frag. 150.9– 10, 17–18). The land of the Ethiopians is where the sun rises and where the sun is situated when the weather is cold up north in Greece; it becomes warmer later for all the Greeks (the Panhellenes).

137. *mortal tripod.* Presumably a mortal tripod is an old person using a cane.

makes an old man into a wheel.[133] He does not blow through a tender-skinned virgin, who inside the house stays at her dear mother's side, not yet experienced in the works of much-golden Aphrodite; she washes her delicate neck well and rubs herself richly with olive oil and lies down inside her room inside the *oikos* on a wintry day, when the Boneless One[134] gnaws his own foot in his fireless *oikos* and sorry abode, for the sun does not show him a pasture to set out for. Rather, the sun visits the territory[135] and *polis* of the Dark Men[136] and shines rather later on the Panhellenes. And just then, the horned and unhorned woods-dwellers, their teeth chattering miserably, flee through the thickets in the glens, and this is a concern for all in their chests: how in their search for shelters they may get hold of close-packed hiding places within a rocky recess. Just then, they are like a mortal tripod,[137] whose back is broken forward and whose head looks at the threshold. Like that one they wander, avoiding the white snow.

536   And at that time don a defense for your skin, as I exhort you, both a soft cloak and a hemmed tunic: weave a thick woof on a thin warp. Don this so that your hairs may

138. *body.* This word, *soma,* in Homer and elsewhere in Hesiod, only means "dead body." Aristarchus first remarked on this fact in the third century B.C.E. Presumably, though curiously, it refers to a living body here.

139. *kindly times that bring help. euphonai,* "kindly times," must be a euphemism for "nights," further euphemized by *epirrothoi,* "help-bringing."

140. *balance your nights and days.* We presume that this means that one monitors the relative lengths of the days and nights, providing more food daily as the nights become shorter.

keep still and not bristle, lifted straight up over your body.[138] Bind round your feet fitted boots from an ox slain in its prime, after lining the inside with felt. When the cold comes in its season, stitch together the hides of firstborn kids with the sinew of an ox, to throw it round on your back as a protection from rain. On your head above wear a snugly made felt cap so that rain may not soak your ears. For dawn is ice-cold when Boreas has attacked, and the mist of dawn over the earth from starry heaven is spread over the wheat-bearing works of blessed men, a mist that has drawn water from ever-flowing rivers and has been lifted high over the earth by a squall of wind: sometimes it rains toward evening, at other times it blows, when Thracian Boreas drives the close-packed clouds. Conclude your work and set out for your *oikos* before Boreas [comes], lest sometime a dark cloud from heaven cover you over and make your skin dripping wet and soak your clothes: avoid that. For this is the hardest month: wintry, hard on the livestock, hard on people.

559   At this time let there be half food for the oxen, but better than half the food ration for your man; for the kindly times that bring help[139] are long. Watching for these things until the year's completion, balance your nights and days,[140] until in turn Earth, mother of all, bears her varied produce again.

141. *turnings of the sun.* See above, note 120. We are now in late February.

142. *the star Arcturus.* Arcturus seems to circle around the Great Bear, hence his name, "Bear-Watcher." Note that Arcturus is rising here in twilight (an acronychal rising). Most risings and settings referred to by Hesiod are those observed in the sky just before daybreak. We call these "daytime" risings, appearances, etc.

143. *daughter of Pandion.* Pandion is an early Athenian king, whose long-suffering daughter, Procne, was metamorphosed into a nightingale, not a swallow. This indicates either an independent tradition for the metamorphosis or a mistransmission of it by Hesiod.

144. Oikos-*Carrier.* This is another kenning as riddle: the snail, although there are presumably other possible guesses, such as the tortoise.

145. *When the golden thistle blooms.* It is June now.

146. *women at their lewdest, and men at their weakest.* This reflects a perhaps widely held belief among the Greeks that women's lust was connected with summer's heat. Aristotle comments on the subject, quoting Hesiod:

> Why are men less capable of sexual activity in the summer,
> but women more so, as the poet says about thistle-blooming
> time, "women are at their lewdest, and men at their weakest"?
> Is it because the testicles hang down more than in the winter?
> But it is necessary for a man to draw them up if he intends
> to engage in sexual activity. Or because hot characteristics fail
> from excessive heat, while cool ones thrive? It is true that
> a man is dry and hot, a woman cool and moist. And so the

564   When Zeus completes sixty wintry days after the turnings of the sun,[141] at just that time the star Arcturus[142] leaves behind the holy stream of Ocean and ascends for the first time, beaming brilliantly at earliest twilight. After him, the dawn-wailing swallow, the daughter of Pandion,[143] rises into the light for people when spring is just beginning. Cut back the vines before the swallow; for thus is it advisable.

571   But once the *Oikos*-Carrier[144] climbs from the ground onto the plantings, as he flees the Pleiades, just then it is no longer cultivating time for vines: sharpen the sickles and rouse the slaves. Steer clear of seats in the shade and of lying in bed until dawn at reaping time, when the sun withers the skin. At that time hurry and bring the produce to the *oikos:* rise at dawn, and there may be sufficient sustenance for you. For dawn supplies a one-third share of your work; dawn advances a man on the road and advances him in his work; when she has appeared, dawn sends many people on their way and puts yokes on many oxen.

582   When the golden thistle blooms,[145] and the shrill cicada, sitting in a tree, often lets fall its fine singing from under its wings, in the season of laborious summer, then are goats fattest, wine at its best, women at their lewdest, and men at their weakest,[146] when Sirius parches the head and the knees, and the skin is dried from the heat. But then let

power of a man is diminished, while that of a woman thrives, for it is balanced by its opposite. (*Problems* 879a27–35)

In humans the male feels the urge for intercourse more in the winter, the female in the summer. (*Historia animalium* 542a33–542b1)

147. *bibline wine.* This may be wine made from papyrus, although in the fifth century B.C.E. there is firm evidence of a wine by this designation named for a district in Thrace (north of Greece).

148. *brisk Zephyr.* The Zephyr was the refreshing west wind of springtime, here hoped for in summer.

149. *Orion.* Orion was transferred to the heavens as a constellation because he unwisely pursued Artemis, virgin goddess of the hunt. His first daytime appearance in Hesiod's time was about June 20.

150. *put your worker out of the* oikos. The other (equally possible) meaning is "engage a worker who has no *oikos*," the very opposite! But the instructive point here is that a worker (*thes*) was dependent for work on the seasons. The *thes* was the lowest of all orders in early Greece, for he did not belong to an *oikos*. This low status makes Achilles' words in the Underworld so poignant: "I would rather work the land for another man as a *thes,* even for a man who had no holding (*kleros*), for a man who had hardly any livelihood, than be ruler over all the corpses that are dead" (*Odyssey* 11.489–491).

151. *day-sleeping man.* He means a thief.

152. *reach heaven's middle.* This is what the Greek says, but what is meant is that Orion and Sirius are due south in the sky at dawn. How Hesiod and his neighbors might calculate this is unclear. "Middle" became a technical term for "south" in Latin as

me have shade from a rock and bibline wine[147] and emmer
soaked in milk and milk from goats that are going dry and
the flesh of a cow fed in the woods, not yet a mother, and of
firstborn kids. Further, let me drink blazing wine, sitting in
the shade, having satisfied my heart with food, after turning
my face into brisk Zephyr.[148] Let me pour three [measures]
of water from an ever-flowing, running, unmuddied spring,
and add a fourth of wine.

597   Urge your slaves to thresh out Demeter's holy grain,
whenever strong Orion[149] first appears, in an airy place and
on the well-rolled threshing floor. With a measuring scoop
give heed to [storing] it well in vats When you have put
away all your sustenance under lock inside your *oikos,* I exhort
you to put your worker out of the *oikos*[150] and to search for
a hired girl without a child; a hired girl with a child at her
breast is hard. Tend also to your jagged-toothed dog—do
not stint on his bread—lest a day-sleeping man[151] seize your
goods. Bring in fodder and litter that you may have an abundance for the oxen and the asses. But then have the slaves
cool off their poor knees and set loose the oxen pair.

609   When Orion and Sirius reach heaven's middle,[152]

well (Latin *meridies* means "noon" as well as "south," which is where the sun is at noon where Hesiod lived).

153. *and rose-fingered Dawn looks upon Arcturus.* The daytime rising of Arcturus in Hesiod's time was about September 9.

154. *Hyades.* The Hyades are located in the head of the constellation Taurus. Hesiod elsewhere (frag. 291) names them Phaesyla, Coronis, Clea, Pheo, and Eudora. They set in Hesiod's morning on November 4. Like the Pleiades, the Hyades are associated with rain; their name may be derived from the verb *huein,* "to rain," or the noun *hus,* "pig" (cf. their Latin name, Suculae, "piggies").

155. *wine-dark.* This is Homer's famous adjective *oinops.* What it is supposed to mean has been a source of contention for millennia. It has been suggested that it was originally a word that indicated the time of day, "sunset-red" (Rutherford-Dyer 1983).

156. *wings.* These are sails, boats being regularly compared to birds. It is possible that Hesiod here is actually talking about putting away the oars.

157. *steering oar up in the smoke.* Recall that above (45) Hesiod told us that one could put one's steering oar up "soon" if a sufficient livelihood were an easy thing to accomplish. If a livelihood were an easy thing to come by, one would not have to go to sea at all.

and rose-fingered Dawn looks upon Arcturus,[153] O Perses, then pluck [and take] all the grape clusters to the *oikos,* and expose them to the sun for ten days and ten nights, put them in shade for five days, and on the sixth day decant the gifts of much-cheering Dionysus into vats. But when the Pleiades and the Hyades[154] and strong Orion are setting, right then be mindful of plowing in season; then may the seed be well lodged under the ground.

618 If desire for stormy seamanship seizes you: when the Pleiades, fleeing Orion's powerful strength, fall into the misty open sea, at just that time do the blasts of winds of all kinds rage. Then no longer keep your ships on the wine-dark[155] open sea, but be mindful to work the land, as I exhort you. Draw your ship onto dry land and surround it with stones on all sides, to keep out the damp might of the blowing winds; do this after you have drawn out the bilge plug, so that the rain of Zeus may not cause it to rot. Put all the equipment away under lock in your *oikos,* after trimming in orderly fashion the wings[156] of the open-sea-going ship; hang the well-worked steering oar up in the smoke.[157]

630 You yourself wait for sailing time, until it comes; then drag your swift ship to the sea and furnish on board a fitting cargo in order to gain a *kerdos* [and bring it] to the *oikos.* Just so my father and yours, Perses, you utter fool,

158. kerdos *on top of* kerdos. "*kerdos* on top of *kerdos*" is the same syntactical idiom as "work upon work"; repetitive actions lead to cumulative results.

159. *trade.* Trade is *emporie*—literally, the activity of being a traveler (*emporos*) on a ship that is carrying goods to be exchanged. Some portion of any ship's contents probably belonged to one or more *emporoi* (who were not necessarily on board). Hesiod does not himself go to sea.

160. *except to Euboea from Aulis.* Such a trip involves only about a hundred yards of "seafaring." Euboea is the large island off the east coast of Greece, Aulis the place on the mainland where the Greek heroes gathered in anticipation of their trip to Troy to fetch Helen. With this narrative Hesiod at first equates himself with the Homeric heroes by going to Aulis, but then he separates himself from them by sailing only a hundred yards, instead of all the way to Troy. Thus Hesiod emphasizes that he is different from Homer (Nagy 1982, 66; also Rosen 1990).

161. *Achaeans.* Achaeans is the primary name that Homer used to designate the Greek warriors who laid siege to Troy.

162. *Chalcis.* Chalcis was one of the two great cities of Euboea; Eretria was the other. Both (often together) were leading players in the new trading activities of the eighth century and subsequently.

163. *tripod.* Tripods were used both for ritual burnings in temples and other holy places and for prizes at competitions (singing and athletic).

164. *poem.* This may be a reference to his *Theogony,* an ingenious theory first proposed by H. T. Wade-Gery (1949, 87). He is followed by West (1966, 44–45) and Janko (1982, 94).

used to sail in ships, because he was in need of a good livelihood. Once he came here in his black ship, after making it
across much open sea, having left behind Aeolian Cume. He
was not fleeing riches, wealth, and prosperity, but the evil
poverty that Zeus gives to men. He settled near Helicon in a
pitiful village, Ascra, bad in the winter, painful in the summer, never any good.

641 Perses, be mindful of all works in their season, especially as regards seamanship. Praise a little ship, but put your
cargo in a big one; the greater the cargo, the greater will be
the *kerdos* on top of *kerdos*,[158] if the winds hold back the evil
blasts.

646 Whenever you turn your witless spirit to trade[159]
and wish to evade *chrea* and delightless hunger, I will indeed
point out to you the rules of the much-roaring sea, although
I am in no way skilled in either seamanship or ships. For, as
for ships, I have never yet sailed on the wide open sea, except
to Euboea from Aulis,[160] where the Achaeans[161] once waited
through the winter and gathered together from holy Greece
a great host against Troy of the fair women. At that time I
traveled over into Chalcis[162] for the contests of warlike Amphidamas; the greathearted one's sons had announced and
set up many prizes. There, I boast, I won an eared tripod[163]
with a poem[164] and carried it off. I dedicated it to the Muses

165. *fine singing.* Hesiod narrates this event at *Theogony* 22–34:

[The Muses] once taught Hesiod fair song, when he was
shepherding his sheep under holy Helicon. First the goddesses
spoke this word to me: "Rustic shepherds, base reproaches,
mere bellies, we know how to speak many falsehoods that are
like truths, but we also know, when we wish, how to pro-
nounce truths." So spoke the articulate daughters of great
Zeus. And they gave me a scepter, a shoot of healthy laurel, a
marvelous thing they had plucked. And they breathed into me
divinely inspired song, so that I might celebrate both the future and the past. And they bade me celebrate the generation
of the blessed ones who are forever, and always to sing them
themselves first and last.

166. *Beginning fifty days after.* Traditionally this passage is
translated "for fifty days after," i.e., the sailing time is the period
of fifty days after the solstice. We follow G. L. Snider's revisionist
interpretation (1978), plausible in the Greek and in keeping with
what we know about wind patterns in the eastern Mediterranean.

167. *Poseidon.* Zeus's brother, Poseidon is a versatile god whose
concerns include the sea, horses, and earthquakes.

168. *Notus.* Notus is the name of the south wind, the opposite
of Boreas.

of Helicon, where they first sent me on the road of fine sing-ing.[165] That much experience with many-doweled ships I have had, but even so I will tell to you the purpose of Zeus the Aegis-Mover, for the Muses taught me to sing an incom-parable poem.

663   Beginning fifty days after[166] the turnings of the sun, when summer, the laborious season, has come to its end, that is the sailing time for mortals. Neither would you wreck your ship nor would the sea lay men to waste, unless indeed Poseidon the Ground-Shaker[167] is bent on it, or Zeus, *basileus* of the deathless ones, sees fit to destroy them; for in these gods is the end, equally, of good things and of bad. At that time the breezes are well defined, and the open sea is without disaster. Then without anxiety entrust your swift ship to the winds, drag it into the open sea, and put all your cargo in it. Then hurry as quickly as you can to get back to your *oikos;* do not wait for the new wine and the summer rain, winter's onset and the terrible blasts of Notus,[168] who accompanies the heavy summer rain of Zeus; Notus stirs up the sea and makes the open sea hard.

678   There is another sailing time for people, in the spring. Just when first a leaf on the top of a fig branch ap-pears to a man as big as the track that a crow makes when he walks, then the sea is ready for climbing on board your ship:

169. *goods are life breath for wretched mortals.* We do not think that this statement tells us much about precisely what Hesiod is giving or getting in his "trading" activities. Likewise, it seems unlikely (though certainly attractive) that Hesiod is saying that "trading" is necessary for survival. Rather, Hesiod is commenting on the human tendency to accumulate goods.

170. *it is terrible if . . . come to nothing.* Hesiod is not changing subjects (nor taking a wagon to sea!). He is talking about the trip to the coast with his goods in his wagon: too many goods may mean no cargo on the ship at all. That said, it is not inconceivable that Hesiod's wagon is a metaphor for the ship.

171. *Watch out for your amounts.* Or "take due measure (as in all things)."

172. *right degree.* This is a translation of *kairos,* which is the opposite of "excess"; it is the middle road (Wilson 1980, 179). At line 329, "against what is proper" is a translation of *parakairia,* literally, "contrary to *kairos.*"

173. *neither very much . . . marrying time.* This is a view held also by later Greeks. In the sixth century the Athenian Solon (27.9) recommended that men marry between twenty-eight and thirty-five. In the fourth century, Plato in various passages recommended age ranges of twenty-five to thirty-five and thirty to thirty-five; Aristotle offered thirty-seven. For references see West's note.

174. *marry in the fifth.* Plato suggests sixteen to twenty; Aristotle about eighteen. See West.

that is the sailing time in spring. I myself don't praise it, for it is in no way welcome to my spirit; it has to be snatched; you would steer clear of evil with difficulty; but out of ignorant thinking, people do these things, for goods are life breath for wretched mortals.[169] It is a terrible thing to die among the waves. But I command you to consider all these things in your chest, as I argue.

689 Do not put your entire substance in hollow ships, but leave most behind, and load less. It is terrible to encounter a disaster in the waves of the open sea; it is terrible if, by lifting an excessive load onto your wagon, you should wreck the axle and the cargo come to nothing.[170] Watch out for your amounts;[171] the right degree[172] on every occasion is best.

695 Take your wife into the *oikos* when you are the right age, neither very much short of thirty years nor much beyond that: that is marrying time.[173] Let a bride be four years past puberty; let her marry in the fifth.[174] Marry a virgin in order that you may teach her devoted ways, and marry especially one who resides near you, after looking carefully at all things around you, lest you marry a source of laughter for the neighbors. For a man carries off nothing better than a good wife, and in turn there is nothing else more chilling than an evil one, a meal-ambusher who scorches her hus-

175. *is willing to provide* dike. Here, finally, is a case where *dike* refers to an offer from one party to a second party without judgment from a third. Even if there is no specific offer being made here, but rather the expression of a willingness to make amends or to "set things right," we are still looking at a solution without a third party.

band without a firebrand, even though he be strong, and gives him over to raw old age.

706 Watch well for the vengeance of the deathless blessed ones.

707 Do not make a companion equal to a brother. But if you do, do not do him an evil turn first, and do not lie for your tongue's pleasure. If he does you an evil turn first, either by speaking some offensive word or by deed, remember to pay back twice as much. But if he invites you again into friendship and is willing to provide *dike,* accept it.[175] Wretched is the man who makes now one man, now another man his friend. Do not let your thinking contradict your appearance.

715 Do not be called overly hospitable nor inhospitable, nor a companion of evil men nor a wrangling maker against good men. And do not ever dare to reproach a man for his destructive, spirit-wasting poverty, a gift of the blessed ones who are forever. The best treasure among people is that of a thrifty tongue; the greatest pleasure is that of a tongue that moves in orderly fashion. If you should say something evil, you yourself would quickly hear more [of the same]. And do not be stormy at a well-attended feast; pleasure is greatest and cost the smallest when the feast is shared by the community.

176. *And do not ever . . . nor in springs.* These and the following lines may be construed as a display of sensitivity to the perils of contaminating sources of fresh water with human wastes (Hughes 1975, 51; 1994, 52). This sentence (through "advisable course") survives in the manuscript as lines 757–759; we have followed West in moving them to follow lines 736. They clearly belong here.

177. *pollution.* This is *kakotes,* earlier translated "failure." It is the noun from the connotatively neutral adjective *kakos,* "evil."

178. *cut the withered from the living from the five-branched one with burning iron.* We have here a riddle of sorts: do not pare your nails at the dinner table. In early Greek poetry, iron is routinely "burning" (*aithon*), and wine, bronze, and hunger are routinely "blazing" (*aithops*).

724   And do not ever pour blazing wine to Zeus at dawn with unwashed hands, nor to the other deathless ones; for they do not heed such prayers and spit them back. Do not urinate standing straight up and turned toward the sun; but, when it is setting until it is rising, remember not to strip yourself, and piss either on the road or off the road as you walk: nights belong to the blessed ones. A godly man, who knows wise things, is one who does it squatting or after he has walked over to the wall of a well-fenced courtyard. And do not spill semen on your genitals inside your *oikos* and show it off next to the fireplace: avoid doing it. Procreate your offspring after coming back home, not from an ill-omened funeral, but from a feast for the deathless ones.

And do not ever piss in the waters of rivers that flow to the sea nor in springs:[176] especially avoid doing this, and do not shit there, for it is not an advisable course.

And do not ever pass through the fair-flowing water of ever-flowing rivers on foot until you have looked into the fair streams, washed your hands in the pellucid, very desirable water, and then prayed. Whoever crosses a river not having washed the pollution[177] from his hands, him the gods resent, and they give him pains thereafter. At a plentiful feast for the gods do not cut the withered from the living from the five-branched one with burning iron.[178] And do

179. *caw.* A crow's caw on the rooftop was believed to be a harbinger generally of bad luck, specifically of bad weather (see West): therefore, if you could prevent the caw, you could avert the bad luck or weather.

180. *brought to pass.* This is not clear. Immovable things may be, but are not certainly, tombstones; but if not tombstones, we have no idea what else. This appears to be a prescriptive reference to circumcision, an emphatically non-Greek practice. One must conclude that these lines, although they contain culturally alien information, are perceived by Hesiod as worth passing on.

181. *sacrifices.* The Greek merely says "holies" or "holy things," but we presume these to be sacrifices. The god mentioned at the end of the line is the god in whose honor the specific things are burning.

182. Lines 765–828. Here begins the section that is probably reflected in the poem's title: these are the "Days." Many scholars have considered this a later accretion to the text, although it was not thought so in antiquity. It is our position that this section does not need to be considered a later accretion, but that it should probably be taken as something of a set piece, for it contains material that could not be of practical interest to Hesiod and his presumed audience. For example, they did not use horses.

183. *sorting out the truth.* The Greeks sorted out (verb *krinein*) the signs that they read in the natural world, coming up with guidance after acquiring sufficient information. Often the information came from birds like the crow on the rooftop (above, line 747); Hesiod will mention bird sorting below at lines 801 and 828.

not ever put the wine ladle on top of the mixing bowl when men are drinking, for a deadly destiny is brought to pass out of that. And when building a house do not leave [the roof] unsmoothed, lest a screaming crow sit down on it and caw.[179] And do not eat and do not wash with what you have taken from undedicated legged caldrons, since there is a penalty also in these actions. And do not set a twelve-day-old boy on immovable things, for it is not an advisable course: it makes a man manless; nor a twelve-month-old: this same thing is brought to pass.[180] And a man ought not to clean his skin with a woman's bathwater, for there is a sorry penalty for a time also in that. And if you should encounter burning sacrifices,[181] do not criticize what is being consumed: the god resents that also.

760 Do these things, and avoid the wretched talk of mortals, for talk is evil, lightweight, and very easy to lift, but painful to carry and hard to put aside. No talk that many people talk perishes completely. Talk herself is a kind of goddess.

765[182] Watching out well for the days that come from Zeus, point them out properly to your slaves. The thirtieth day of the month is best for inspecting works and for distributing the food ration; it is the day that people spend sorting out the truth.[183]

184. Lines 769ff. Hesiod employs three different methods of referring to the days of the month. Sometimes he counts days consecutively up to thirty; at other times, he divides the month into three parts and speaks of days within each third or decade; he also speaks of the part of the month when the moon is waxing (translated as "the beginning of the month" at lines 780 and 798) and waning ("the end" at line 798), which implies a two-part month. (Some cities later counted the third decade backwards; we cannot be sure whether Hesiod does or not.) Many Greek cities employed multiple systems, and most operated independently of the others. It has been argued that this portion of *Works and Days* was designed to make the disparate methods uniform from *polis* to *polis* (Nagy 1988). For more on the Greek calendar, see Bickerman 1980, 27–28, 99–100.

185. *Wise One.* This is another riddling kenning, probably the ant. It may be quite literally a wise person.

769[184]   For these days are from Zeus the Planner: to start out, the first and the fourth and the seventh are each a holy day—for on the seventh Leto bore Apollo of the golden sword—and so are the eighth and the ninth. Nevertheless, two days above the others of the beginning of the month are good for toiling at mortal works: the eleventh and twelfth. Both are good, both for shearing sheep and for reaping the happy produce, but the twelfth is much better than the eleventh, for on it the high-soaring spider spins his webs at midday, when the Wise One[185] reaps his heap. On this day have your woman set up her loom and arrange her work in front of herself.

780   Avoid the thirteenth of the beginning of the month for starting the sowing. For getting plantings bedded in, however, it is the best day.

782   The middle sixth is especially unsuitable for plantings, but a good day for a male to be born. It is not suitable for a girl either to be born at all or indeed to take a share of marriage.

785   The first sixth day is not fitting for a girl to be born; rather it is a favorable day for castrating kids and flocks of sheep, and for throwing up a pen for the sheep flock; it is a good day for a male to be born; but such a boy would be

186. *knower.* The Greek word is *histor* (in Homer, *istor*). A man who effectively decides wranglings (*neikea*) is an *istor* (on the Shield: *Iliad* 18.501 [see the Introduction, p. 47]); an arbitrator in a dispute or the man who holds the stakes for a wager would be an *istor* (Agamemnon at *Iliad* 23.486). A *histor* in Thespiae may be involved in Hesiod's wrangling with Perses.

187. *the fourth of . . . the end.* We would be tempted to say that by this Hesiod means the twenty-seventh rather than the twenty-fourth, were it not the case that Hesiod brings up the twenty-seventh later in some detail (814–818).

188. *Erinyes . . . Horkos . . . Eris.* The Erinyes are the furies who exact penalty from forswearers. Horkos we met above as Oath (219). Eris is here the bad Strife, described above (14–16; see note 4), and distinguished there from the good Strife. Again, since the "Days" section of the poem appears to be more or less a set piece, there should be no problem with the reversion to a singular Eris here.

fond of speaking taunts and lies and wheedling words and hidden conversations.

790   On the eighth of the month castrate the boar and the loud-bellowing ox, but do the work-enduring mules on the twelfth.

792   On the great twentieth, at midday, is born a knower:[186] he will be especially expert in intellect.

794   The tenth is a good day for a male to be born, while the middle fourth is good for a girl. On that day tame the sheep and the twisted-horned oxen of shambling gait and the jagged-toothed dog and the work-enduring mules, putting your hand to them. In your spirit watch out to avoid the fourth of both the beginning and the end[187] for devouring your spirit with pains; it is a day especially so ordained.

800   On the fourth of the month lead a wife into the *oikos* after sorting out the birds that are best for this action.

802   Avoid fifths, since they are hard and dreadful, for on the fifth they say that the Erinyes acted as attendants as Horkos was being born, whom Eris[188] bore as a disaster for forswearers.

805   On the middle seventh, watching very carefully, throw Demeter's holy grain on the well-rolled threshing floor, and have the woodcutter cut beams for rooms and many ship timbers such as are fit for ships.

189. *horses.* They would be yoked not for field work or for pulling a wagon—the horse collar would not be invented for better than 1,500 years—but for travel in a chariot. Hesiod had no horses.

190. *call it by its true name.* Few people call the twenty-seventh by its true name, which is "thrice-nine."

191. *Beyond all others . . . a holy day.* This assertive tone seems to indicate that what was the case later, that four was a lucky number, did not universally obtain in Hesiod's time.

192. *know the after-twenty.* Few people know the true name of the twenty-first, which is "after-twenty."

193. *of changeable thunder.* This is a wonderfully elegant choice of adjective that survives in the Greek language only here. Something of changeable thunder is (presumably) of indeterminate omen, neither good nor bad.

809   On the fourth start to build narrow ships.

810   The middle ninth day is better toward evening.

811   The very first ninth is entirely without disaster for people: it is a good day for conceiving and for being born, for male and female both, and it is never a totally bad day.

814   Again, few men know that the thrice-nine of the month is best for starting a jar and for putting the yoke on the neck of your oxen and asses and swift-footed horses,[189] and for drawing your many-benched, swift ship into the wine-dark open sea; few men call it by its true name.[190]

819   On the fourth, open a jar. Beyond all others the middle fourth is a holy day.[191] Again, few men know the after-twenty[192] of a month, which is best as dawn is coming; it is worse toward evening.

822   These days are a great boon for men on the ground; the others are of changeable thunder,[193] doomless, bringing nothing at all. Different persons praise different days, but few really know. Sometimes a day is a stepmother, at other times it is a mother. As regards these days, fortunate and prosperous is he who knows all these things and does his work guiltless before the deathless ones, sorting out the birds and avoiding excesses.

WORKS CITED

〜〜〜〜

Akurgal, Ekrem. 1983. *Alt Smyrna*, Vol. 1, *Wohnschichten und Athena-tempel*. Ankara: Türk Tarih Kurumu Basimevi.

Andrews, Mary E. 1943. Hesiod and Amos. *Journal of Religion* 23: 194–205.

Andreyev, V. N. 1974. Some aspects of agrarian conditions in Attica in the fifth to third centuries B.C. *Eirene* 12: 5–46.

Athanassakis, Apostolos N., trans. 1983. *Hesiod: Theogony, Works and Days, Shield*. Baltimore: Johns Hopkins University Press.

Baden-Powell, B. H. 1892. *The land-systems of British India*. Oxford: Clarendon Press.

Bailey, F. G. 1957. *Caste and the economic frontier: A village in highland Orissa*. Manchester: Manchester University Press.

Bickerman, E. J. 1980. *Chronology of the ancient world*. Rev. ed. Ithaca, N.Y.: Cornell University Press.

Bintliff, John L. 1985. The Boeotia survey. In *Archaeological field survey in Britain and abroad*, edited by Sarah Macready and F. H. Thompson, 196–216. London: The Society of Antiquaries of London.

Bohannan, Paul, and Laura Bohannan. 1968. *Tiv economy.* Evanston, Ill.: Northwestern University Press.

Bravo, Benedetto. 1977. Remarques sur les assises sociales, les formes d'organisation et la terminologie du commerce maritime grec à l'époque archaique. *Dialogues d'Histoire Ancienne* 3:1–59.

Burnett, Ann Pippin. 1991. Signals from the unconscious in early Greek poetry. *Classical Philology* 86:275–300.

Buxton, Richard. 1994. *Imaginary Greece: The contexts of mythology.* Cambridge: Cambridge University Press.

Camp, John McK., II. 1979. A drought in the late eighth century B.C. *Hesperia* 48:397–411.

Carlier, Pierre. 1984. *La royauté en Grèce avant Alexandre.* Strasbourg: AECR.

Coldstream, J. N. 1977. *Geometric Greece.* New York: St. Martin's.

Cooper, Alison Burford. 1977–78. The family farm in Greece. *Classical Journal* 73:162–75.

Crotty, Kevin. 1982. *Song and action: The victory odes of Pindar.* Baltimore: Johns Hopkins University Press.

Darcus, Shirley M. 1979. A person's relation to *phren* in Homer, Hesiod, and the Greek lyric poets. *Glotta* 57:159–73.

Detienne, Marcel. 1963. *Crise agraire et attitude religieuse chez Hésiode.* Brussels: Latomus.

Dodds, E. R. 1951. *The Greeks and the irrational.* Berkeley: University of California Press.

Donlan, Walter. 1970. Changes and shifts in the meaning of DEMOS in the literature of the archaic period. *La Parola del Passato* 25:381–95.

———. 1973. The tradition of anti-aristocratic thought in early Greek poetry. *Historia* 22:145–54.

———. 1985. The social groups of dark age Greece. *Classical Philology* 80:293–308.

———. 1989. Homeric *temenos* and the land economy of the Dark Age. *Museum Helveticum* 46:129–45.

Drews, Robert. 1983. *Basileus: The evidence for kingship in Geometric Greece*. New Haven: Yale University Press.

Duncan, Colin A. M., and David W. Tandy, eds. 1994. *From political economy to anthropology: Situating economic life in past societies*. Montreal: Black Rose Books.

Farron, S. G. 1979–80. The *Odyssey* as an anti-aristocratic statement. *Studies in Antiquity* 1:59–101.

Fine, John V. A. 1983. *The ancient Greeks: A critical study*. Cambridge, Mass.: Harvard University Press.

Finley, Moses I. 1978. *The world of Odysseus*. 2d rev. ed. London: Penguin.

Francis, E. K. L. 1945. The personality type of the peasant according to Hesiod's *Works and Days*. *Rural Sociology* 10:275–95.

Fränkel, Hermann. 1951. *Dichtung und Philosophie des frühen Griechentums: Eine Geschichte der griechischen Literatur von Homer bis Pindar*. Philological Monographs, no. 13. New York: American Philological Association. (2d ed.: *Dichtung und Philosophie des frühen Griechentums: Eine Geschichte der griechischen Epik, Lyrik und Prosa bis zur Mitte des fünften Jahrhunderts* [Munich: C. H. Beck, 1962]; translation: *Early Greek poetry and philosophy: A history of Greek epic, lyric, and prose to the middle of the fifth century*, trans. Moses Hadas and James Willis [New York: Harcourt Brace Jovanovich, 1975].)

Frazier, R. M., trans. 1983. *The poems of Hesiod*. Norman, Okla.: University of Oklahoma Press.

Gagarin, Michael. 1973. *Dike* in the *Works and Days*. *Classical Philology* 68:81–94.

———. 1974. Hesiod's dispute with Perses. *Transactions of the American Philological Association* 104:103–11.

———. 1986. *Early Greek law*. Berkeley: University of California Press.

———. 1992. The poetry of justice: Hesiod and the origins of Greek law. *Ramus* 21.1:61–79.

Garnsey, Peter. 1988. *Famine and food supply in the Greco-Roman world.* Cambridge: Cambridge University Press.

———. 1992. Yield of the land. In *Agriculture in ancient Greece,* edited by Berit Wells, 147–53. Stockholm: Paul Åströms Förlag.

Garnsey, Peter, and Ian Morris. 1989. Risk and the *polis:* The evolution of institutionalised responses to food supply problems in the ancient Greek state. In Halstead and O'Shea 1989, 98–105.

Gernet, Louis. 1981. *The anthropology of ancient Greece.* Translated by John Hamilton and Blaise Nagy. Baltimore: Johns Hopkins University Press.

Gow, A. S. F. 1914. The ancient plough. *Journal of Hellenic Studies* 34: 249–75.

Green, Peter. 1984. *Works and days* 1–285: Hesiod's invisible audience. In *Mnemai: Classical studies in memory of Karl K. Hulley,* edited by H. D. Evjen, 21–39. Chico, Calif.: Scholars Press.

Halstead, Paul. 1987. Traditional and ancient rural economy in Mediterranean Europe: Plus ça change? *Journal of Hellenic Studies* 107: 77–87.

———. 1989. The economy has a normal surplus: Economic stability and social change among early farming communities of Thessaly, Greece. In Halstead and O'Shea 1989, 68–80.

Halstead, Paul, and Glynis Jones. 1989. Agrarian ecology in the Greek islands: Time stress, scale and risk. *Journal of Hellenic Studies* 109: 41–56.

Halstead, Paul, and John O'Shea, eds. 1989. *Bad year economics: Cultural responses to risk and uncertainty.* Cambridge: Cambridge University Press.

Halverson, John. 1985. Social order in the *Odyssey. Hermes* 113: 129–45.

———. 1986. The succession issue in the *Odyssey. Greece and Rome* 33: 119–28.

Hamilton, Richard. 1989. *The architecture of Hesiodic poetry.* Baltimore: Johns Hopkins University Press.

Hansen, Mogens Herman, ed. 1993. *The ancient Greek city-state.* Historisk-filosofiske Meddelelser, vol. 67. Copenhagen: Royal Danish Academy of Sciences and Letters.

Hubbard, Thomas K. (Forthcoming.) Hesiod's fable of the hawk and the nightingale reconsidered. *Greek, Roman and Byzantine Studies.*

Hughes, J. Donald. 1975. *Ecology in Ancient Civilizations.* Albuquerque: University of New Mexico Press.

———. 1994. *Pan's travail: Environmental problems of the ancient Greeks and Romans.* Baltimore: Johns Hopkins University Press.

Janko, Richard. 1982. *Homer, Hesiod and the Hymns: Diachronic development in epic diction.* Cambridge: Cambridge University Press.

de Jong, Irene. 1987. Homeric *kerdos* and *ophelos. Museum Helveticum* 44:79–81.

Lamberton, Robert. 1988. *Hesiod.* New Haven: Yale University Press.

Lattimore, Richmond, trans. 1959. *Hesiod: The Works and Days, Theogony, The Shield of Herakles.* Ann Arbor: University of Michigan.

Lenz, John. 1993. Kings and the ideology of kingship in early Greece (c. 1200–700 B.C.): Epic, archaeology and history. Ph.D. diss., Columbia University.

Lichtheim, Miriam. 1976. *Ancient Egyptian literature: A book of readings.* Vol. 2, *The New Kingdom.* Berkeley: University of California Press.

Lombardo, Stanley, trans. 1993. *Hesiod: Works and Days and Theogony.* Notes and glossary by Robert Lamberton. Indianapolis: Hackett.

Lonsdale, Steven F. 1989. Hesiod's hawk and nightingale (*Op.* 202–212): Fable or omen? *Hermes* 117:403–12.

Magagna, Victor V. 1991. *Communities of grain: Rural rebellion in comparative perspective.* Ithaca, N.Y.: Cornell University Press.

Marquardt, Patricia. 1984. Hesiod's *Op.* 464: Gaia as "soother of children." *Classical World* 77.5:297–99.

Martin, Richard P. 1984. Hesiod, Odysseus, and the instruction of princes. *Transactions of the American Philological Association* 114: 29–48.

———. 1992. Hesiod's metanastic poetics. *Ramus* 21.1:11–33.

Mayhew, Anne, Walter C. Neale, and David W. Tandy. 1985. Markets in the ancient Near East: A challenge to Silver's argument and use of evidence. *Journal of Economic History* 45:127–34.

Mele, Alfonso. 1979. *Il commercio greco arcaico: Prexis ed emporie.* Cahiers du Centre Jean Bérard, no. 4. Naples: Institut Français de Naples.

Millett, Paul. 1984. Hesiod and his world. *Proceedings of the Cambridge Philological Society* 210 (n.s. 30): 84–115.

Montet, Pierre. 1981. *Everyday life in Egypt in the days of Ramesses the Great.* Translated by A. R. Maxwell-Hyslop and M. S. Drower. Philadelphia: University of Pennsylvania Press.

Morris, Ian M. 1987. *Burial and society: The rise of the Greek city-state.* Cambridge: Cambridge University Press.

Nagy, Gregory. 1982. Hesiod. In *Ancient writers: Greece and Rome,* vol. 1, edited by T. James Luce, 43–73. New York: Charles Scribner's Sons.

———. 1988. The pan-hellenization of the "days" in the *Works and days.* In *Daidalikon: Studies in honor of Raymond V. Schoder, S.J.,* edited by Robert F. Sutton, 273–77. Chicago: Bolchazy-Carducci.

Neale, Walter C. 1962. *Economic change in rural India: Land tenure and reform in Uttar Pradesh, 1800–1955.* New Haven: Yale University Press.

Neale, Walter C., and David W. Tandy. 1988. Review of *Economic structures of the ancient Near East,* by Morris Silver. *Journal of Economic History* 48.2:442–43.

Onians, R. B. 1951. *The origins of European thought about the body, the mind, the soul, the world, time, and fate.* Cambridge: Cambridge University Press.

Oppenheim, A. Leo. 1954. The seafaring merchants of Ur. *Journal of the American Oriental Society* 74:6–17.

————. 1977. *Ancient Mesopotamia*. Rev. ed., completed by Erica Reiner. Chicago: University of Chicago Press.

Phillips, J. H. 1980. The "boneless one" in Hesiod. *Philologus* 124: 152–54.

Polanyi, Karl. 1944. *The great transformation*. New York: Rinehart.

————. 1957. Marketless trading in Hammurabi's time. In Polanyi, Arensberg, and Pearson 1957, 12–26.

————. 1960. On the comparative treatment of economic institutions in antiquity, with illustrations from Athens, Mycenae and Alalakh. In *City invincible,* edited by Carl H. Kraeling and Robert McC. Adams, 329–50. Chicago: University of Chicago Press.

————. 1963. Ports of trade in early societies. *Journal of Economic History* 23:30–45.

————. 1977. *The livelihood of man*. New York: Academic.

Polanyi, Karl, Conrad M. Arensberg, and Harry W. Pearson, eds. 1957. *Trade and market in the early empires*. Glencoe, Ill.: Free Press.

Popham, M. R., and L. H. Sackett. 1968. *Excavations at Lefkandi, Euboea, 1964–1966*. London: Thames and Hudson.

Popham, M. R., L. H. Sackett, and P. G. Themelis, eds. 1980. *Lefkandi*. Vol. 1, *The iron age*. London: Thames and Hudson.

Raaflaub, Kurt A. 1993. Homer to Solon. The rise of the *polis:* The written sources. In Hansen 1993, 41–106.

Redfield, James M. 1991. Classics and anthropology. *Arion* n.s. 1.2: 5–23.

Redfield, Robert. 1953. *The primitive world and its transformations*. Ithaca, N.Y.: Cornell University Press.

————. 1956. *Peasant society and culture*. Chicago: University of Chicago Press.

Renehan, Robert. 1980. Progress in Hesiod. *Classical Philology* 75: 339–58.

————. 1987. Review of Verdenius 1985. *Gnomon* 59.7:577–80.

Reverdin, O., ed. 1962. *Hésiode et son influence*. Fondation Hardt, vol. 7. Geneva: Fondation Hardt.

Revere, Robert B. 1957. "No man's coast": Ports of trade in the eastern Mediterranean. In Polanyi, Arensberg, and Pearson 1957, 38–63.

Richardson, N. J. 1979. Review of West 1978. *Journal of Hellenic Studies* 79:169–71.

Richardson, N. J., and S. Piggott. 1982. Hesiod's wagon: Text and technology. *Journal of Hellenic Studies* 102:225–29.

Rose, Peter W. 1975. Class ambivalence in the *Odyssey. Historia* 24: 129–49.

Rosen, George. 1975. *Peasant society in a changing economy: Comparative development in southeast Asia and India.* Urbana: University of Illinois Press.

Rosen, Ralph M. 1990. Poetry and sailing in Hesiod's *Works and days. Classical Antiquity* 9:99–113.

Rutherford-Dyer, R. 1983. Homer's wine-dark sea. *Greece and Rome* 30:125–28.

Rzach, Alois. 1958 [1902]. *Hesiodi carmina.* Reprint of 1913 third ed. of original ed. of 1902, Leipzig: Teubner.

Sallares, Robert. 1991. *The ecology of the ancient Greek world.* Ithaca, N.Y.: Cornell University Press.

Schiering, Wolfgang. 1968. Landwirtschaftliche Geräte. In *Die Landwirtschaft im homerischen Zeitalter,* Archaeologia homerica, vol. 2h, edited by Will Richter, 147–58. Göttingen: Vandenhöck and Ruprecht.

Silver, Morris. 1983. Karl Polanyi and markets in the ancient Near East: The challenge of the evidence. *Journal of Economic History* 43:795–829.

———. 1986. *Economic structures of the ancient Near East.* Totowa, N.J.: Barnes and Noble.

Smithson, Evelyn Lord. 1968. The tomb of a rich Athenian lady, ca. 850 B.C. *Hesperia* 37:77–116.

Snider, G. L. 1978. Hesiod's sailing season [W&D 663–664]. *American Journal of Ancient History* 3:129–35.

Snodgrass, Anthony M. 1971. *The dark age of Greece.* Edinburgh: Edinburgh University Press.

———. 1977. *Archaeology and the rise of the Greek state.* Cambridge: Cambridge University Press.

———. 1980. *Archaic Greece: The age of experiment.* Berkeley: University of California Press.

———. 1991. Archaeology and the study of the Greek city. In *City and country in the ancient world,* edited by John Rich and Andrew Wallace-Hadrill, 1–23. London and New York: Routledge.

———. 1993. The rise of the *polis:* The archaeological evidence. In Hansen 1993, 30–40.

Solmsen, Friedrich. 1949. *Hesiod and Aeschylus.* Ithaca, N.Y.: Cornell University Press.

———, ed. 1990. *Hesiodi Theogony Opera et Dies Scutum.* 3d ed. of original 1970 ed. Oxford: Oxford University Press.

Starr, Chester G. 1977. *The economic and social growth of early Greece, 800–500 B.C.* New York: Oxford University Press.

———. 1982. Economic and social conditions in the Greek world. In *The Cambridge Ancient History,* 2d ed., vol. 3, pt. 3, 417–41.

———. 1986. *Individual and community: The rise of the Polis, 800–500 B.C.* New York: Oxford University Press.

Tandy, David W. 1997. *Warriors into traders: The power of the market in early Greece.* Berkeley: University of California Press.

Tandy, David W., and Walter C. Neale. 1994. Karl Polanyi's distinctive approach to social analysis and the case of ancient Greece: Ideas, criticisms, consequences. In Duncan and Tandy 1994, 9–33.

Thomas, Carol G. 1978. From wanax to basileus: Kingship in the Greek dark age. *Hispania Antiqua* 6:187 206.

Ulf, Christoph. 1990. *Die homerische Gesellschaft: Materialien zur analytischen Beschreibung und historischen Lokalisierung.* Munich: C. H. Beck.

Verdenius, W. J. 1980. Review of West 1978. *Mnemosyne* 33:377–89.

———. 1985. *A commentary on Hesiod, Works and Days, vv. 1–382.* Leiden: E. J. Brill.

Vernant, Jean-Pierre. 1983a [1960]. Hesiod's myth of the races: An essay in structural analysis. In *Myth and thought among the Greeks,* 3–32. French original in *Revue de l'Histoire des Religions* 157: 21–54.

———. 1983b [1966]. Hesiod's myth of the races: A reassessment. In *Myth and thought among the Greeks,* 33–72. French original in *Revue de Philologie* 40:247–76.

Wade-Gery, H. T. 1949. Hesiod. *Phoenix* 3:81–93.

Watkins, Calvert. 1978. ἀνόστεος ὅν πόδα τένδει. In *Étrennes de septantraine: Travaux de linguistique et de grammaire comparée offerts à Michel Lejeune,* 231–35. Paris: Éditions Klincksieck.

Wender, Dorothea Schmidt, trans. 1973. *Hesiod and Theognis.* Harmondsworth: Penguin.

West, Martin L., ed. and comm. 1966. *Hesiod: Theogony.* Oxford: Oxford University Press.

———, ed. and comm. 1978. *Hesiod: Works and Days.* Oxford: Oxford University Press.

West, Martin L., trans. 1988. *Hesiod: Theogony and Works and Days.* Oxford: Oxford University Press.

Wilamowitz-Moellendorff, Ulrich von, ed. 1928. *Hesiodos Erga.* Berlin: Weidmann.

Will, Edouard. 1957. Homère, Hésiode et l'arrière-plan Mycenien. *Revue des Études Anciennes* 59:5–50.

Williams, Bernard A. O. 1993. *Shame and necessity.* Berkeley: University of California Press.

Wilson, J. R. 1980. Kairos as "due measure." *Glotta* 58:177–204.

Wink, André. 1986. *Land and sovereignty in India: Agrarian society and politics under the eighteenth-century Maratha svarajya.* Cambridge: Cambridge University Press.

Wolf, Eric R. 1966. *Peasants.* Englewood Cliffs, N.J.: Prentice-Hall.

INDEX

〰〰〰

Generosity, 37

Grains: estimates of yields, 29–30; fear of crop failure, 33; possible importing of, 35; storage of, 33–35

Hesiod: as peasant and farmer, 25–26; as *persona,* 7–8; as poet, 6–7; size of his *oikos,* 27–31; varying theories of his identity, 26–27

Homer: Hesiod in shadow of, 2; as poet, 7

Household. *See oikos*

Hunger: linked with debt, 33, 40–41

Ischia: western end of trade routes, 13, 14

Justice. *See dike*

kerdos: and debt, 41; as "gain," 36–37

kleros: as "lot," 25

Labor: division of, 28–29

Land tenure. *See* Alienation; Debt

Law. *See dike*

Lefkandi: leading settlement in Dark Age, 11; storage at, 34

Legal action, 46–47; brought by Perses, 4, 42

Markets: relative importance, 23–25

Mycenaean civilization: characterized, 9–10; collapse of, 10–11; Linear B writing, 10

Neighbors: increasing reciprocity among, 37

neikos. See Legal action

oikos: fundamental unit of production, 25; size of Hesiod's, 27–31; tools of, 31–33

Old Smyrna: storage at, 34

Peasantry: Hesiod as typical peasant, 26–27

Perses: Hesiod's advice to, 1; legal action against Hesiod, 4, 42; lost his *oikos,* 39, 47; his problem his own fault, 48; sharing inheritance with Hesiod, 25; urged to be rid of debts, 41. *See also* Debt

Poets: contexts of recitations, 6–7

polis: Greek city-state, 5; ideology of, in Homer and *Theogony,* 19–21

Population: decrease after Mycenaean Age, 10–11; increase in eighth century, 11–13

Port of trade, 24

Reciprocity: among neighbors, 37

Redistribution, 22–23

Seasonal activities, 37–38

Slaves: on small *oikos,* 29

Society: changes in eighth century, 13; distribution of wealth, 14–15; generosity in, 37; organization of, 4–5

Storage, 33–35

Technology: of *oikos,* 31–33

Theogony: Hesiod's earlier poem, 6, 7; nature of, 7

Tools: of *oikos,* 31–33

Trade: always outside community, 36–37; gain from, 36; Hesiod's, 35–37; in Hesiod's time, 23–25; lack of role of prices, 36; routes, 14–15; by sea, 35. *See also* Al Mina; *basileus;* Ischia; *kerdos*

Wealth. *See* Society

Works and Days: date of composition, 1, 4; structure, 3–5

Writing: changes nature of poetry, 6; Linear B, 10; reintroduction and freezing of epic poems, 16

Yields: of grains, 29–30

Designer:	Barbara Jellow
Compositor:	G & S Typesetters, Inc.
Text and Display:	Adobe Garamond
Printer and Binder:	Malloy Lithographing, Inc.